A Taste of Mauritius

A Taste of Mauritius

Paul Jones   *Barry Andrews*

MACMILLAN

A Taste of Mauritius
Paul Jones and Barry Andrews

© Paul Jones and Barry Andrews 1980, 1982
First published 1980 by Editions de I'Ocean Indién Ltée,
Moka, Mauritius.

New edition 1982

Published by Macmillan Education
London and Basingstoke

*Companies and representatives in Lagos, Zaria, Manzini,
Nairobi, Singapore, Hong Kong, Delhi, Dublin, Auckland,
Melbourne, Tokyo, New York, Washington, Dallas*

ISBN 0 333 34005 1 Paper
      0 333 34004 3 Cased

Printed in Hong Kong

Contents

Preface

This is the first Preface I have ever been asked to write for a cookery book. But I must say, in all modesty, that the invitation came as no surprise. International jet-setters may be ignorant of the fact (they tend to be a bit ignorant when it comes to facts what with all their dashing about and being lagged most of the time) but it is widely accepted where I live (the poor quarter of the County of Surrey, England) that I am to oriental *haute cuisine* what Dame Margot Fonteyn is to non-ferrous sheet-metal welding.

I am happy to contribute this Preface because the book itself was cobbled together (literary jargon meaning 'meticulously researched and endlessly rewritten until perfection has been achieved') by two young men in the hotel line of business whom I know well from my visits to the Saint Géran Hotel, Mauritius.

When the soft life in affluent, prosperous England begins to pall my wife and I have taken to coming out to stay at the Saint Géran for a few days of frugality and self-denial. Our Spartan regime begins when we leap out of bed at 10 am. This we force ourselves to do whatever the weather is like, even if there is a suggestion of cloud lurking over Curepipe. We have a simple breakfast. However seductive the smell of crispening bacon and hot croissants wafting across from the grill we never queue up and go round again more than three times. Most of the day is spent working our way through a schedule of exercises, eg, half an hour floating in the lagoon, a brisk work-out hurling crumbs to a bulbul, another float, a steady jog all round the beach parasol and back, another float, a brisk walk across the bridge to the pool bar . . . Rigorous? Perhaps. But self-discipline is good for the soul, and we work up a cracking appetite for dinner.

And what dinners. I think we have tasted most of the delights described in this book at one Saint Géran meal or another, including the boat sculpted out of ice and the margarine dodo (see 'Barbecue Displays; food as an art form'). It was at a beach barbecue and we were not supposed to attack the decorations but in the dark I did not realise that they were sculpted and knocked a bit off the rudder of the ice boat to cool a half coconut-shell of liquid dynamite which had gone warm in the tropical night air. A little while later I passed a knife across the dodo's knee in order to butter a prawn which I was holding. Quite why I wanted to butter the prawn I do not recall but I do remember that I was talking animatedly at the time to a lady croupier in a long yellow dress slit to her ear.

It is clear from the above notes that *A Taste of Mauritius* conveys the flavour of a way of life which is a little different from that of, say, Birmingham, New Jersey, Hillbrow, Rouen or Woolahra. Certainly the food is different. 'Good' hotels in England tend to have a menu which is a square metre in size, almost no customers, a defeated pianist playing 'Gems from Oklahoma' and depressingly pretentious food. Everything is stuffed with something else, eg, Trout stuffed with Prawns stuffed with Paté, or Breast of Chicken stuffed with Tomatoes stuffed with Rice. The meal is (eventually) served by either a local youth with terminal acne and enormous red hands or an incredibly aged waiter who mutters to himself. It is no good complaining to the chef because it is quite clear from the food that he cooked it before he went off duty at 3 pm and it has been subsequently reheated by Mrs Hackett who helps out in the kitchen and used to be on Room Service before her leg went.

Paul Jones and Barry Andrews, the authors of this book, arrange matters rather differently. Paul Jones manages the Saint Géran but, instead of being a worried figure in black jacket and striped trousers lurking behind Reception with the air of a man wanting to get home and rewire the electric kettle before his wife gets home, he is always around the hotel, dressed like a guest (better dressed than some of us) and clearly happy to sit down and talk, or eat, or just sit. He gives the appearance of a man who really likes his hotel.

And Barry, the chef — foolhardy at the least, you might think, and suicidal at the worst — actually appears at mealtimes. No furtive chef he, peering through the round window of the kitchen door and mouthing 'He's eaten it!'. He strolls openly amongst the diners, soliciting criticism, enjoying the sight of people eating, ever ready with a jug of iced water should a newly arrived guest take a too sudden forkful of Chicken Curry and cry out that his neck has caught fire.

I recommend this book to you.

It is just possible that there might be a reader who has read this far and would like to say to me: 'Is it not true that this is not a Preface to a book of recipes at all but a description instead of the two authors and the hotel in which they work? And is this not because you do not know a good recipe from a hole in the ground and are hoping that Paul Jones and Barry Andrews are so good at their jobs that the recipes must be good?'

I have, of course, a complete and dignified answer to both these accusations:

Yes.

FRANK MUIR

Delicious Mauritius

Arriving in Mauritius is like suddenly finding oneself in an oven in which a rich fruitcake has just risen. Warmth and exotic aromas are everywhere.

The islands of the Mascarenes were formed very much like confectionery. Chopped and churned, creamed and kneaded, then heaved like heavy dough from the depths of a primordial ocean towards a tropical sun. In the heat of that volcanic moment rocks, like raisins, were thrown heavenward, molten syrups poured from every fissure, and pungent vapours filled the blazing sky.

Mauritius found itself cooling down on a choice stretch of the Indian Ocean on the 20th parallel just north of the tropic of Capricorn. The white ash with which its crust had been sprinkled blew away and the elements, like an erratic pastry chef, tweaked the smouldering surface into funny shapes.

The rest of the story reads like a remake of *Genesis*. Warm breezes brought the seeds of plants and trees that sprang into tropical forests on landing in the rich volcanic soil. Birds floating past on their way to yet uncharted destinations stopped by. Some of them stayed and were nationalised. The dodo stayed so long that it forgot to fly. The black parrot too discovered the joys of walking. Giant tortoises popped their heads out of the water, blinked, and decided to go amphibious. Insects stuck out feelers, were impressed, and crawled into the sun to mutate and multiply. In the depths of the forest a huge bat stirred. In the meantime primordial bubbles, intent on turning into polyps and unable to scramble ashore like the rest, decided to set up camp within eye-shot of this paradise isle. Thus a coral reef was formed around Mauritius. Island and reef remained untouched for several millennia.

The first glimpse of Mauritius by the human eye was possibly a blue speck on the horizon viewed by the captain of an Arab dhow, too busy whizzing past in brisk south-east trades to stop. However, he remembered to dot his map in the appropriate place. *Diva mashriq* he called it, meaning Eastern Isle.

The Eastern Isle must have welcomed Man's first appearance in 1510 with the predicament of a vestal virgin on her first night out — a mixture of trembling trepidation and secret joy. It was her fears rather than her hopes that were ultimately confirmed. The Portuguese got as far as naming the island *Cirne*, the swan, but didn't do much else. Why they chose that name is a little baffling since amidst all the birdlife that by now existed the swan certainly did not figure. If the dodo had been the inspiration, then the Portuguese equivalent of ugly duckling might have been more appropriate. One likes to think that it was the purity and elegance of the landscape which won the island its second name.

If the Portuguese had sinned by omission, the Dutch who arrived in 1598 were active offenders. They razed the black ebony forests and felled the palm trees. They also sat down to huge feasts of barbecued dodo. But they didn't like it much. They called it *walghvogel* — nauseous bird with the tough, unpalatable flesh. They also called it *doudo*, simpleton. Doudo's were understandably simple. One gets like that, wandering starry-eyed through idyllic landscapes for centuries. One's faculties begin to drop off, one's wings to shrivel and one's defence mechanisms to require overhauling. It becomes a trifle difficult without tooth, claw, wing or inventive to frighten off sailors' dogs when they are about to devour your eggs — sunny side up. So you surrender to your fate and wait for the time when you will be immortalised by the stories of Lewis Carroll and on the proud emblem of the Mauritian nation.

In 1710, the Dutch abandoned a dodoless and semi-denuded island. In exchange they left behind a small but valuable legacy — a name that was to be revived, Mauritius, after Maurice de Nassau, a crop that was to be the island's lifeblood, sugar-cane, and a herd of Javanese deer that was to provide food and sport for generations of hunters and gourmets.

When the Dutch left, the island became the haunt of marauding pirates. They had set up headquarters in Madagascar, which they called Libertalia. Mauritius was one of the branches. The pirates did everything expected of them — plundered, pillaged, bit cutlasses, walked the plank and consumed huge quantities of Mauritian rum. One of them even carried off a Mongolian princess in true Hollywood fashion. The most interesting aspect of their activities remains the treasure that they buried — marcs, ryals, sterling silver objects, gold ingots and chunks of raw diamond. People are still digging.

The arrival of the French on the Indian Ocean colonial scene was in connection with Bourbon (now La Réunion and still French), and Rodrigues (now a dependency of Mauritius). In 1689 ten French Huguenots landed in Rodrigues. They had a great time living on exotic fruit and vegetables, oysters and turtles, fish and spiny lobsters. With a typical French sense of priorities, they immediately began to distil a first-class wine from the juice of palm trees. Things were beginning to resemble a *Club Mediterranée* when someone noticed the shortage of women. It was the need for female companionship that caused those ten stalwart Frenchmen actually to brave the seas, and Dutch authority, and row in the direction of Mauritius — 320 miles away. When after eight days they staggered ashore, it was the sight of cows rather than of Dutch ladies which caused them to jump with joy. They hadn't drunk fresh milk for several years and proceeded to do so minutes after disembarking. The Dutch were highly suspicious, imprisoned them and then sent them packing to France — via Java.

But the Frenchman isn't put off that easily. He returned twenty-two years later in the person of Dufresne d'Arsel, the captain of a ship carrying coffee plants to Bourbon for the

first time. When he got to Mauritius there was no opposition. The Dutch had left five years earlier. So he raised the tri-coloured flag, drank a toast and re-christened the island Isle de France.

The early French administrators did very little except choose Port Louis as the main harbour. Today it is the capital. Then in 1745, Mahé de Labourdonnais took over as governor. He had become a sailor by the age of ten and a prosperous trader by twenty-one. He had sailed the seas off India and China, becoming a dab hand at anti-pirate warfare. Louis X thought he was just the man to get things going in the Isle de France. He was dead right. Labourdonnais rebuilt Port Louis, put down rebellions, introduced cassava or *manioc* (this became the staple food of the slaves) and opened the first sugar mill. But he had to leave Mauritius to fight the British in India. He captured Madras but was accused of pocketing the ransom money. He spent two years in the Bastille on charges of bribery.

Labourdonnais, however, had laid firm foundations, and over the hundred odd years of French rule the island became a fairly prosperous agricultural, commercial and military centre. Spices failed to grow but sugar continued to do well. Some of the sugar was fermented into arrack — a potent liquor and an absolute necessity when the sight of sea, sun and sand begins to pall. The island at this time attracted seafarers and scholars, navigators and novelists — even Irishmen. When the news of the French Revolution reached Isle de France the island was under the control of two Irishmen with French nationalities — Conway and Macnamara!

One novelist who was attracted to the Isle de France was Bernardin de St Pierre. He was an engineer turned *raconteur*. At twelve, fascinated by Defoe's *Robinson Crusoe*, he travelled to the West Indies. Among his adult achievements are the post of royal engineer to Catherine of Russia, the post of professor of moral philosophy, a discharge from the Corps of Engineers for insubordination, and the writing of the most popular 'Love Story' of the time — *Paul et Virginie*. He was on his way to Madagascar when he discovered Isle de France. He stayed for two years. He was so inspired by the primitive beauty of the island and the 'noble savage' temperament of its people that he wove an imaginative tale of young love and death against the social and natural background of the Isle. The wreck of the *Saint Géran*, an historical fact, was the starting point around which the story was moulded.

The story is a study in simplicity, pathos and the exotic. It is about two women who are bonded together in friendship through common problems and preoccupations. One is widowed before giving birth to a daughter, Virginie; the other has been abandoned by her lover and left with a young son, Paul. Paul and Virginie are brought up by their mothers and faithful slaves. They grow up together in innocence and purity, as children of the good earth. It is the unspoilt beauty of the Isle de France that brings out Paul and Virginie's natural goodness. The two mothers look forward to the day when their children's innocent affection

will blossom into conjugal love. But things begin to go wrong when Virginie is persuaded by Governor Labourdonnais to leave for Paris to be educated by a wealthy aunt. Virginie is miserable in France, in surroundings so different from the natural haunts of her childhood days. She turns down a profitable marriage and can only think of Paul and her island home. She finally decides to return to Isle de France. But the ship in which she is travelling, the *Saint Géran*, is smashed to pieces on the reef. Virginie, too modest to undress and be saved by a naked sailor, is washed overboard. Paul tries to save her but is thrown up on the shore, bleeding and unconscious. Two months later he dies of a broken heart.

The novel is a wonderful social document on Isle de France in the eighteenth century. It shows us how families planted millet and maize, rice and pumpkins, sweet potatoes, cucumber and courgettes, sugar-cane on hard ground and coffee on the hillsides. They even grew their own tobacco. Once, when the lovers are lost in the forests of Black River, they eat wild watercress from the river. Then Paul ingeniously burns down a palm tree to obtain a heart of palm — still a Mauritian delicacy today. When they are finally found by slaves, they are refreshed and strengthened with '*un gâteau, des fruits et une grande calebasse remplie d'une liqueur composée d'eau, de vin, de jus de citron, du sucre et de muscade*'. Virginie's specialities were sorbets and cordials made from sugar-cane juice, lemons and limes — a concoction that many a contemporary barman might wish to try out.

By the turn of the century Britain was beginning to make furtive bids for the island that bore France's name. They succeeded in 1810. In August of that year they tried to hammer the French on water. A small British fleet under an eccentric, Captain Willoughby, lured French ships into the bay of Grand Port by raising the French colours. Once enemy ships were inside the reef, the French flag was replaced by the Union Jack and battle commenced. But it was a dismal failure for the British. Willoughby lost an eye, and the battle of Grand Port. He and his French adversary, Duperré, ended up convalescing in the same house, in an early gesture of *entente cordiale*. It didn't last. The British tried again to possess the island, this time by land. They marched on Port Louis on the 3rd December 1810 and it fell.

The island was renamed Mauritius and became a Victorian colony. But the French language, culture and judicial system were allowed to continue. The sugar industry flourished, slavery was abolished, there was an influx of Indian labourers, the Chinese started arriving, and some of the diverse ingredients of the present-day Mauritian cocktail began to appear and to be gently stirred, not shaken. The glacé cherry, which came as the final crowning touch, was Independence from Britain in 1968.

Present-day Mauritius retains much of the magical quality of its pre-human days. That magic — a fusion of innocence, primary colours and fauvist simplicity — is encapsulated in the paintings of the contemporary Mauritian artist, Malcolm de Chazal. Lobsters still talk to the mountains, crabs still dance on the sands in a flurry of legs and claws, and families of pineapples drip colour on to the red earth like pigment off a paint-brush. Admittedly, deer tracks are now dual carriage ways, and the marsh where the dodo frolicked now houses Plaisance International Airport. But the volcanic rock mountains, churned up by titanic forces

 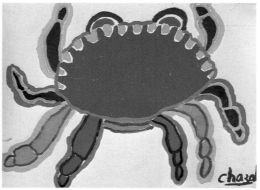

and chiselled by wind and weather, still stand, as stunning as the day the Portuguese first set eyes on them. These mountains have inspired comment from a number of astute observers: 'jagged tooth-like volcanic stumps'; 'pocket size Matterhorns'; 'toy summits'; 'blue pinnacled apparitions, almost transparent'; 'haunting shapes which a giant axe seems to have carved in the basalt'. The peaks, which are not lofty (the highest does not exceed a thousand metres), form a kind of prickly backbone, a watershed from which glistening waterfalls tumble and flow into rivers. There are wide fertile plains to the north but, as one moves south, one is lifted gently on to a plateau. It reaches its climax in wooded gorges and ravines, buttresses, escarpments and dizzy peaks, then descends again quickly to the foaming south coast. In an island totalling about 2000 square kilometres, topographical variety of this kind is as dramatic as the backdrop for a Wagnerian opera.

The forested gorges are thick with eucalyptus, ebony, camphor, sisal, travellers' palm, tambalacoque, Indian almond and Chinese guava. The undergrowth of knotted grass, privet, creeper and fern often hides indigenous orchids so rare as to be still unclassified. The air is aquiver with multitudinous insects, as benign and beautiful as the dragonflies suspended from the trees by invisible wires. On the outskirts graze the Javanese deer and Malaysian monkeys

screech from the tree tops. Charles Darwin once walked these forests collecting specimens and murmuring to himself, 'How pleasant it would be to pass one's life in such quiet abodes'.

The forest is also a natural bird sanctuary for ring-necked parakeets, fodies, olive and grey white-eyes, cardinals, cuckoo-shrikes, bulbuls, swiftlets and red-tailed tropic birds. The tropic bird, with its long straw tail (*paille-en-queue*), will, if you wave a white handkerchief, nose-dive at you with terrifying speed and accuracy. If you glimpse a Mauritius kestrel (*mangeur de poule*) swooping down over the valley, you will have seen the rarest bird in the world. The pink pigeon is also fighting for survival.

Below sea level is the enchanted universe of marine creatures, coral flowers, waving seaweed, rolling meadows of seagrass, mysterious caves, spiky urchins, scuttling shells, motionless sea slugs, fish that glare contemptuously as they tickle you with their tails, fish that speed past you in a perpetual performance of *Giselle*. Locked into nature-made reserves by the coral reef, huge communities of myriad fish burst upon you like firework displays. In the deep blue waters beyond the reef lurk the sharks, the blue and black marlin, the sailfish and the swordfish. All these come in king-size varieties, which makes Mauritius one of the few places on earth where fishing stories *can* be believed.

Shells associated with Mauritius include an unusual variety of map cowrie, a unique violet spider conch, the rare volute anna and the largest specimen of aulicus cone ever found. One of the rarest Mauritian shells is the double or imperial harp. The number of ribs on the last whorl of the body is double the number found on the more common single harp. Find a colony of double harps and you need never fish for your supper again.

Shells, coral and rock are pounded by the breakers on the reef into powder as fine as talc, then washed up on shore to form white beaches. Shoals of parrot fish nibbling away at the reef with their powerful beaks and emitting sprays of coral particles also contribute to keeping the beaches dazzle bright. The beaches are curved like seedless watermelons with a thick rind of tropical greenery running along the edge where the casuarina trees end and the coral sands begin. The sands in turn gently subside into the generous, luscious lap of the Indian Ocean.

The Indian Ocean that surrounds Mauritius is not simply a part of the tropical habitat, it is much more. It has had a moderating and enlightening influence on national character and turned Mauritians into a carefree, tolerant and welcoming people. The sea has become symbolic of the island's openness to the outside world. The long sequence of seafaring colonisers has left behind broadmindedness and adaptability. From very early times the island has been on the trade routes between East and West. The Mauritian people themselves have come to the island across the oceans from the four quarters of the globe. The peopling of Mauritius has been described as 'a series of overlapping waves of immigration, each wave bringing with it new customs and languages'. The wave image is particularly appropriate.

The French came in their schooners from France and neighbouring Bourbon. The slaves came in brigs from Mozambique and Madagascar. Muslim traders sailed from western India to establish trade links with Mauritius. Indian artisans from southern India came to help build Port Louis harbour, and Indian labourers came to keep the sugar industry going once the slaves had been emancipated. Early records show the presence of Chinese settlers in Mauritius as early as 1783, but bulk immigration only started in the 1890's. They came from mainland China and Hong Kong and soon became successful retailers and businessmen.

All this has resulted in a heady brew of races and cultures and a delightful mixed salad of languages. Road signs are in English, newspapers are in French. English is the official language, the language of education, of job interviews, of law courts, of the Legislative Assembly, of income tax forms. Hindi is heard a great deal on radio and television. Urdu, Tamil and Telegu speakers are also catered for. Bhojpuri is spoken in many villages. Prices in some shops are notched up in Chinese. Bargaining takes place in Creole. Creole is the *lingua franca*. It is largly French-based but borrows freely from Portuguese (*camarons*, freshwater prawns), from Malagasy (*tandrac*, hedgehog), from Chinese (*min*, flour noodles) and from the Indian languages, (*gadjak*, snack; *farata*, Indian bread; *masala*, curry powder; *dekchee*, cooking utensil, etc). Mauritians jump from one language to the next like overworked international switchboard operators.

The festivals of Mauritius are the outward manifestation of the cultural diversity. *Cavadee* is a Tamil festival celebrated towards the end of January. *Cavadees,* which are semi-circular wooden frames decked with flowers, green lemons, palm leaves and coconuts, are carried through the streets by processions of saffron-robed devotees. In a radical gesture of self-mortification they pierce their bodies with thin metal spikes, some the size of hairpins, others

as long and lethal as sharpened knitting needles. Dabbed with stripes of white powder paint, bristling with metal from tongue to toe, *Cavadee*-bearers make their way in an impassioned trance to the temple where they pour milk on the statue of Muruga. For *Maha Shivaratree*, the Great Night of Shiva, the Hindus go on pilgrimage to Grand Bassin — a natural lake high on the central plateau. They wear white and carry *kanwars*. These are intricate wooden structures covered in white paper and flashing with the tiny lights of a thousand mirrors. The Muslims go out to sea in boats to glimpse the new moon. If it appears they return to announce the end of a month of fasting and to celebrate, with prayers in the mosque, *Id-Ul-Fitr*. Later in the year they will sacrifice a goat, a sheep or an ox in memory of Abraham. It is the full moon which commands attention during the mid-Autumn festival, when the Chinese pray to the woman on the moon and offer her a delightful selection of tea and cakes. What is even more delightful is the fact that the same Mauritian who prays to the moon, or sacrifices a goat, or walks to Grand Bassin, or carries a *Cavadee,* could well give his family presents for Christmas or chocolate eggs for Easter. In the same way a Christian family will happily light small clay lamps for the Hindu Festival of Light, or let off firecrackers to bring in the Chinese New Year.

It is precisely this juxtaposition of cultures and traditions that makes Mauritius something of a transistorised United Nations. A *gâteau piment* is, despite its name, not remotely related to French pâtisserie — it is made with dholl, saffron and coriander leaves. A wooden mansion in typical French colonial style could well have 'Stratford College' or 'Keats College' writ large over the door. Port Louis theatre is a typical London playhouse, used regularly for the celebration of Indian weddings. A home in the Chinese quarter could display a picture of the 'Sacred Heart' lit by a red Chinese candle. An interior decorated with Indian brass, prints and rugs could include a fine antique *chaise longue* or a Victorian suspension lamp. In addition to small mirrors, *kanwars*, carried in honour of Lord Shiva, are sometimes decorated with glass baubles of the kind usually reserved for Christmas trees. A Creole belle might greet you with a gentle *namasté* gesture, an Indian beauty with kisses *à la parisienne* — on both cheeks. The call of the muezzin mingles with the rattle of mahjong pieces, the sound of the sitar with that of the sega.

The sega is song. The sega is movement and rhythm. The Mauritian word 'sega' probably originates from 'chéga' — a term found in West African dialects meaning 'song'. A heavy rhythm runs through the Mauritian sega, linking it firmly to the African continent. The Creole words of the sega are sometimes melancholic, turning it into a kind of slave song — full of sadness and suffering, dejection and despair. At other times the sega sparkles with wit and eroticism. Words are often improvised so as to poke fun at the dancers or to make the song more topical.

As a dance, the sega is a spontaneous expression of joy and excitement. But it is a carefully controlled dance in which the bare feet of the dancers gently tramp the ground, while the hips move in a graceful, circular way. The men, dressed in striped trousers, loose gaudy shirts and large straw hats, raise their hands in front of them. The women lift their long, brightly-

coloured skirts and flirt with their partners. A woman will not remain with the same partner all evening, but will weave her way through the dancing crowd, revealing her charms to as many suitors as possible. Couples come very close to each other but never actually touch. The dance has all the tensions of a musical tug-of-war.

Only percussion instruments accompany the traditional sega. The *ravane* is the main instrument and is made from goatskin pulled tight over a circular wooden frame. The skin is heated over an open flame, just before the instrument is played, in order to give it better resonance. The *maravane* is a wooden box containing the dried stalks of sugar-cane flowers arranged in upright rows. Running between the rows are dried seeds. When these seeds rub against the stalks they produce a grating sound. The instrument is played by shaking the box horizontally with a rhythmic action. A metal triangle is also struck. It adds a tinkling sound above the boom of the ravane. As evening turns to night, and night to dawn, the full force of the Creole rhythms, and local rum, begin to be felt. That rhythm finally gets the better of the words and music. Spectators are drawn in, share the fever of time present and time past and answer the call of the sega-ravane.

The eating habits of the Mauritians inevitably reflect a cross-fertilised co-existence. Food figures centrally in the different celebrations. Milk and coconut water are often drunk as part of a number of Tamil and Hindu religious ceremonies. An Indian wedding is incomplete without liberal handouts of plastic-packed sweetmeats. For the Telegu New Year, no salty food is eaten — cakes and sweet semolina puddings are the order of the day. The Muslims break their fast with a rich meat or fish *briani* often followed by a sweet vermicelli dish. For Chinese New Year everyone eats *gâteau la cire* (wax cakes). Wine and whole-cooked chickens

are taken to the pagoda as offerings. On Assumption Day, Christians eat a special cake called *Gâteau Marie*. When a child is baptised, little bags of *dragées* (grains of crunchy sugar icing) are distributed to all and sundry. At Christmas, turkeys, pheasant and smoked salmon, flown in from France, appear in the freezers of large supermarkets.

Generally speaking, Mauritians eat more vegetables than meat — most of the meat being imported and rather expensive. Besides, a large number of Mauritians are vegetarian for religious reasons. Vegetables range from the conventional potatoes, onions and carrots to the more exotic *chayote* or *chou chou*, pigeon peas (*embrevades*), aubergines or egg plant, ash and sponge gourd (*patol* and *pipengaille*) and ladies' fingers (*lalo*). Fruit is largely seasonal with the summer months being the best time for abundance and variety. This is when mangoes, lychees, *longans,* watermelons and avocadoes make their gaudy entrance into the market place. Pineapples, bananas and pawpaw are more regularly available. Most Mauritians have a pawpaw tree in their gardens, often leaving the over-ripe fruit to the birds in the air or the snails on the ground. Jak fruit is curried when semi-ripe or eaten *au naturel* when mature. The Jak fruit has been memorably described by Gerald Durrell as 'an obscene green fruit, covered with knobs and looking rather like the corpse of a Martian baby. To help the illusion, there arose from it a thick, sweetish, very pungent smell, vaguely of a putrefying body'. Many Mauritians, and possibly Martians, would disagree.

Mauritians are wonderful at making the most of what is available — a resourcefulness and flair for innovation that manifests itself in many domains other than that of cooking. When he or she comes by some *camarons*, or spears a *calamary*, or splashes out on some *langouste*, you can be certain that the end product always justifies the price or effort. Even the tenrec, a small tailless variety of hedgehog, has fallen into the Mauritian hotpot and emerged a delicacy. What could be simpler or more ingenious than *brèdes* — cooking with the leaves of vegetable plants? Who else has upgraded the rating of the quiet, blushing *pomme d'amour* to that of primadonna? Even the peanut in some recipes gets star status. Because fruit and vegetables tend to be seasonal, Mauritians have developed a tradition of preserves, jams, *compotes* and pickles *(achards)* to remind them of the flavours and fragrances of a season past. The modern freezer has, of course, altered eating habits. For those who can afford it, it has meant that a range of local vegetables is now available all the year round. Similarly, out-of-season wild boar *(cochon marron)* or venison makes appearances in homes and restaurants after a simple bout of defrosting.

That the Mauritian is 'down to earth' in his eating habits is hardly surprising in a country which is essentially agricultural. A dozen *dholl puris*, a type of pancake filled with spicy fresh vegetable chutney and conveniently purchased from a roadside *marchand*, will happily constitute a meal for the whole family. A slice of pineapple or cucumber, dripping with raging red juices prepared by a bicycled vendor, might be lunch for the busy civil servant, businessman or docker. Also on the pavement will be the peanut seller, offering a choice of boiled or grilled peanuts, the former still in their soggy shells, the latter covered in curious shocking-pink skins. The *marchand de pistache* might be chatting to his immediate rival across the street who is sweating over a hot *karahi,* a large pan used for deep frying, in which *samoosas* and *gâteaus piments* are asizzle. Dessert could consist of Chinese guavas — a small red-yellow sweet-sour fruit that grows wild in the forests of Macabé. Dipped in crude salt and chilli powder it is guaranteed to light you up for the rest of the afternoon.

Those lunching away from the streets — in schools and offices, shops and factories, forests and fields, are highly likely to have taken along their *tente*, a small lidded basket with a strap, containing one or more *pains 'maison'*. The *pain 'maison'* was in the old days delivered to the door by mobile bakers, hence the name. It is crusty bread, as round as a big bun, conveniently indented down the middle so that it can be broken exactly in half. It is thus easier to eat — or share! The bread can be consumed with Creole sauce or Indian curry or Chinese sausage or French cheese.

The *pain 'maison'* has been designed for sharing. So too are all the dishes included in this volume for that very purpose. Mauritius has inherited the four great culinary traditions of the world, synthesised them and produced its own. *A Taste of Mauritius* is our way of helping to preserve and proliferate that Mauritian cuisine, for friends and fellow countrymen, within and beyond our shores.

Creole Cooking

the ultimate melting pot

Robin Howe, in *Cooking from the Commonwealth*, writes: 'There are three great kitchens in the world: French, Chinese and Indian.' Mauritians would welcome this opinion, but frown at its limitations. All three cuisines flourish on the island, which of course makes Howe's choice highly acceptable. But the exclusion of Creole cuisine from the top league table wouldn't meet with local approval.

It is true that Creole cooking is relatively recent compared to the time-hallowed culinary traditions of Europe and the Far East. However, Creole food has that distinctive character, vitality and adaptability which makes its contribution to the art of eating widely recognised.

The term 'Creole' was applied originally to people of Spanish ancestry in the southern and central American colonies. But the term has been extended to include persons of mixed ancestry, often involving French and African parentage in places like the Caribbean, some of the southern states of the USA, the Seychelles and the Mascarene Islands.

Creole cooking has developed essentially out of that fusion of black African and European dishes. In Mauritius it has gone one step further. It has incorporated certain qualities of Indian cuisine. Distinct schools of cooking disappear when thrown into the Creole melting pot. What remains is a hot, strong-tasting style of cuisine which makes the most of many worlds.

Brèdes (pages 16 and 24) is a Mauritian dish enjoyed by all, but few could classify it as exclusively Creole or typically Indian. The fact that it is associated with cooking in a number of French colonies tends to favour the Creole connection. But the fact that so many Indians in Mauritius have incorporated it into their daily diet somewhat dims that historical link. *Brèdes* are the leaves of plants fried, mainly with ginger, onions and garlic, and eaten with rice. When stock is added it is eaten as a bouillon. The leaves of watercress (*cresson*), of Indian mustard (*brèdes de Chine*), of Chinese cabbage (*petsai*), of taro or dasheen (*brèdes songe*), of drumsticks (*mouroum*), and of the chayote (*chou chou*) are used. There are also *brèdes martin* and *brèdes malbar*, transalations for which simply do not exist in the English language.

The *chou chou* is frequently used in Mauritian cooking (page 23). It is known in various parts of the world by different names — custard marrow, vegetable pear, cho cho, chuchu, xuxu, christophene, pepinella. It grows in Mexico, the Antilles, Algeria and Mauritius. It is a climbing plant whose pear-shaped fruit are deeply ribbed and spiny. The firm flesh has a delicate flavour.

Another delightful vegetable ingredient, though considerably more revered than *chou chou,* is the heart of palm or *palmiste* (page 19). This is a tender shoot at the crown or top of palm trees. The entire tree is sacrificed to obtain it. Layers of the trunk are peeled away until the precious ivory-coloured core, about two feet long, is reached. The flesh is firm, crisp and delicate beyond description. Records show that even the Dutch, who took possession of Mauritius in 1598, relished *palmiste*. They chopped down whole palm forests to fill their salad bowls. So popular is palm heart now that it spills over from Creole cuisine into French, where it is eaten with Bearnaise sauce (page 175) and into Indian cooking where it is used as a main ingredient for *achard* (page 72). Heart of palm is also used in Caribbean and South American cooking. It is possible nowadays to buy it in tins.

The best Creole meals are eaten in the homes of our fishermen. Fish certainly figures

1. *Sun Fish.   2. Dame Berry.   3. Vieille Rouge   4. Ourite (Pieuvre/Octopus).*
5. *Barracuda (Tazar).   6. Cordonnier.   7. Anguille.   8. Cabot l'herbe.   9. Rouget.*
10. *Vieille Roche.   11. Rouget.   12. Corne.   13. Langouste.   14. Cateau Bleu.*
15. *Cateau Vert.   16. Sea Urchin.   17. Lalo.   18. Mullet.   19. Bourse.   20. Oysters.*
21. *Rouget.   22. Cabot.   23. Flying Fish.   24. Tivieille.   25. Mourgate (Calamar).*
26. *Crab.   27. Camaron.   28. Vacoas.*

prominently in Creole cuisine. The species most appreciated are *sacréchiens*, a superb red deep-water fish, *capitaines* sometimes known as the scavenger, and the *vacoas* or steaker. Other types popular locally are the *cordonnier* (rabbit fish), *carangue* (jack fish) and the *rouget* (red mullet). Giant tuna is fished in deep waters beyond the reef and is used in the well-known and typical *vindaye* (page 17).

Vindaye is what happens when mustard, saffron, chillies, garlic, oil and vinegar, amongst other things, come together and gently seep into the firm flesh of fried tuna. The longer the fish is allowed to soak up the spices, the riper and more potent the *vindaye* becomes. Octopus, known locally as *ourite,* can be subjected to the same battery of ingredients with equally devastating effect. *Vindaye* should be served cold with Creole rice (page 25). The local rum would rekindle rather than extinguish the fire.

It is believed that the name *vindaye* owes its distant linguistic origin to *vin d'ail* — garlic sauce. Similarly, *rougaille* hails from *roux d'ail* — also garlic sauce! Despite etymological connections, and the assertive presence of garlic in both dishes, *vindaye* and *rougaille* are in fact very different even to the innocent palate. A *rougaille,* always served piping hot, has a flavour dominated by the presence of tomatoes — in our case a small tasty variety called *pomme d'amour*. This ingredient, a *force motrice* in most Mauritian Creole cooking, is noticeably absent from *vindaye*.

The pomme d'amour is also the central flavouring and colouring agent in the famous Creole sauce (page 29) — a sauce almost as international as vinaigrette or mayonnaise. Creole sauce, poured over barbecued steak, fired red mullet or boiled prawns, or even eaten on its own with Creole rice, immediately brings a blast of equatorial sunshine to a meal. Adding Creole sauce to an omelette is like turning a funeral cortège into a carnival. Even the placid oyster quivers with excitement at a mere spoonful (page 18).

The French, Chinese and Indians reserve their best dishes for celebrations and festivals. Christmas, Chinese New Year, Eid or Divali would be the occasions for a special meal in the respective ethnic traditions. With Creole cooking this doesn't really happen. Many Mauritians use Creole-type cuisine as part of their daily menu, upgrading a dish by raising the quality or nature of the main ingredient. Hence a family get-together (and this could mean fifty people), occasioned by a fifteenth birthday or baptism, would see the appearance in a *rougaille* or *vindaye* of prawns, fillet steak or a *sacréchien,* rather than the more usual topside. To really celebrate, the Creole cook might roast a turkey, prepare a Muslim briani or eat fried noodles in a Chinese restaurant! That is what living in a plural society is all about.

Bouillon of Drumstick Leaves

Brèdes mouroum en bouillon

Ingredients

1   cleaned onion
2   cloves crushed garlic
10 g crushed root ginger
1   kg brèdes mouroum
1   fish head
2   litres white stock
    oil for frying

Method

Take the leaves from the stalk of the plant using the tender, smaller leaves.
Slice the onions.
Clean the fish head well under running water.
Place the oil in a pan and heat on a moderate fire.
Fry the onions, garlic and ginger for two minutes in hot oil.
Add the fish head and cook.
Stir fry continuously. Do not colour the onions.
Pour the stock over the fish head and cook for one minute.
Add the brèdes mouroum.
Bring to the boil and cook for a few minutes.
Season to taste and serve.
Salt fish may be used instead of the fish head.

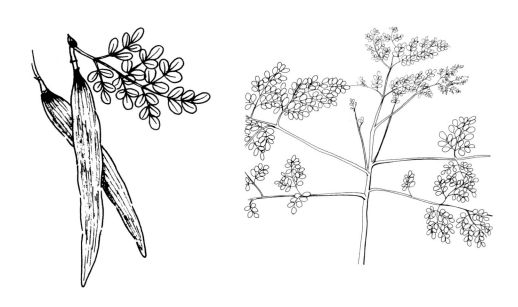

Vindaye of Tuna

Ingredients

5   fillets of tuna
1   large onion cleaned and
       chopped
20 cleaned shallots
20 g mustard seed
20 g saffron
3   green chillies
10 g garlic
10 g crushed root ginger
¼   litre vinegar
1   sprig fresh thyme
       oil for frying
       seasoning

Method

Crush the mustard seeds.
Crush half the garlic with the root ginger.
Leave the rest of the garlic whole.
Cut the chillies in half lengthways.
Add the crushed ginger, garlic and mustard to the vinegar.
Place the oil in a pan and heat it.
Season the fish and place it in the oil to cook.
Remove fish from the pan and fry the shallots and chopped onions.
Add the whole garlic.
Stir the saffron and thyme into the onions. Add the vinegar, mix and stir well.
Cook for three minutes.
Remove from the fire and place the fish into the sauce.
Add the chillies.
Note:
This dish is best served cold with Creole rice and various chutneys. Vindaye can also be made with octopus and venison. Keeping it in the refrigerator for two days improves the flavour.

Oysters Creole Style

Ingredients

oysters
white wine
Creole sauce (page 29)

Method

Open the oysters, clean by removing the beards, place on a tray and season.
Sprinkle white wine over them liberally, sufficient to cover the oysters.
Season and cook in a moderate oven for four minutes. Remove from the oven.
Heat the Creole sauce and spoon over the oysters.
Serve instantly.

Garlic Oysters

Ingredients

	oysters
1	pkt white breadcrumbs
250	g butter
3	cloves crushed garlic
	lemon wedges

Method

Open the oysters, clean by removing the beards, place on a tray and season.
Mix the remaining ingredients into a paste.
Cover the oysters with the garlic butter mix.
Place under grill until breadcrumbs go golden brown.
Serve immediately with lemon wedges.

Palm Heart Creole Style

Ingredients

12 camarons
3   cups Creole sauce
    (page 29)
1   palm heart
    milk

Method

Poach the camarons in a court bouillon.
When cooked, remove and clean.
Cook palm heart in sufficient milk to cover.
When palm heart is soft but firm, remove from the milk and cut into julienne.
Heat the Creole sauce and fold the palm heart into it.
Cut the harder part of the palm bark into portion size pieces. (This is the outer shell that cannot be eaten.)
Place the Creole sauce and palm heart mixture into this shell.
Split the tails of the camarons into two, up to the heads only.
Remove the black veins in their tails.
The camaron heads should then stand upright on the split tails.
Place either side of the palm shells.
Garnish with parsley, spring onion and lemon wedges.
Serve hot.

Beef Rougaille

Ingredients

750 g topside
750 g small fresh tomatoes
3 large sliced onions
20 g grated root ginger
3 cloves crushed garlic
1 sprig fresh thyme
5 g chopped parsley
15 fresh coriander leaves
4 chillies cut lengthways
4 chopped spring onions
    seasoning

Method

Cut the topside into 30 g cubes and season.
Heat the oil in a pan and add the topside to the oil.
Cook for one minute.
Remove the meat from the oil and set aside.
Cut the tomatoes into four.
Add the onions, ginger, thyme, garlic, chillies and the parsley to the oil.
Fry gently on a medium heat for two minutes.
Add the tomatoes and stir in.
Add the beef, stir well and simmer for ten minutes.
Season to taste. Add the spring onions.
Chop the coriander leaves and add half to the mixture.
When about to serve, sprinkle the rest of the coriander on top.
Serve with Creole rice (page 25) and mixed vegetable achard (page 71).
Note:
As an addition finely grated coconut may be added.

Stuffed Pawpaw

Ingredients

1   green pawpaw, medium
     size
20   g finely chopped onions
3   cloves crushed garlic
3   g crushed root ginger
½   kg minced beef
6   chopped tomatoes
3   crushed red chillies
5   g salt
3   g crushed black pepper-
     corns
1   pkt white breadcrumbs
10   g grated cheese
     vegetable oil for frying

Method

Cut the pawpaw in half lengthways and remove the
seeds.
Heat the oil in a pan.
Pre-heat oven to a moderate heat, 350°F (180°C).
Place the onions, garlic and ginger in the oil.
Stir fry for one minute. Do not colour.
Add the beef to the above and stir.
Cook for three minutes.
Add the tomatoes, chillies, salt and pepper.
Stir well and cook for a further two minutes on a fast
heat.
When the mixture has cooled, pour into the pawpaw
shells.
Place the shells in a roasting tin.
Pour water into the tin to the depth of 2.5 cm up
the sides of the pawpaw.
Place in the oven and bake for one hour, covering
with foil if necessary.
Combine the cheese and breadcrumbs.
Remove the pawpaw from the oven and sprinkle the
cheese mix over the top.
Bake again for ten minutes.
The pawpaw should be soft and the top delicately
brown.
Serve hot with Creole sauce (page 29) served
separately.

Venison Creole Style

Ingredients

500 g boneless venison
60   g tomato purée
4   bananas
1   large onion
5   g ground nutmeg
3   cloves crushed garlic
2   teaspoons ground cumin
2   tots brandy
2   tots port
1   litre venison stock
60   g flour
      seasoning
      oil for frying

Method

Peel and chop the onions finely.
Cut the venison into 2.5 cm cubes.
Roll the venison into the flour.
Heat the oil in a pan on a moderate heat.
Fry the chopped onions in the oil for one minute.
Do not colour.
Add the venison and cook for a further two minutes.
Stir in the tomato purée and cook for one minute.
Add the crushed garlic, cumin and nutmeg.
Pour in the venison stock and stir well.
The flour will thicken the stock as it cooks.
Simmer the venison, stirring often, for thirty minutes.
Check if the stock has reduced too much or sauce is too thick. If required, add more stock.
Peel and slice the bananas.
When the venison is tender add the bananas and fold in.
Keep the banana slices whole. Do not break while stirring.
Prior to serving, pour in the brandy and port.
Season to taste.
Serve with Creole rice (page 25).
Grated coconut may be sprinkled on top of the venison.

Chou Chou in White Sauce

Ingredients

1	bayleaf
2	cloves crushed garlic
1	cleaned onion
4	chou chou
30	g flour
30	g butter
1	litre water
3	g nutmeg
½	pkt white breadcrumbs
250	ml milk
	seasoning

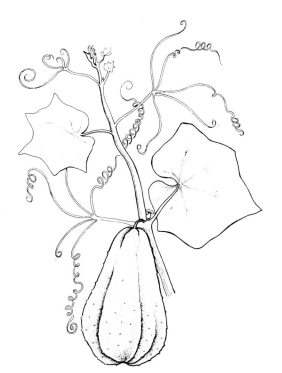

Method

Put the water into a pan with the bayleaf and cloves and bring to the boil.

Place the chou chou in the water and cook until tender but firm. Remove from the water.

Peel, cut in half to remove the stone and slice the chou chou.

Mix the butter and flour together to form a soft paste. Add the garlic to the paste.

Place this in a pan on a moderate heat.

Pour in the hot chou chou water stirring all the time. Stir well to form a smooth sauce. Add the milk and stir.

More milk may be needed to bring the sauce to the correct consistency.

Season to taste and add the nutmeg.

Place the sliced chou chou on a plate.

Cover the chou chou with the sauce and sprinkle with white breadcrumbs.

Grated cheese may be added to the sauce for extra taste.

Cheese may also be blended in with the breadcrumbs before putting the dish under the grill.

Brèdes Touffé

Ingredients

1 kg brèdes
4 cloves garlic
5 g root ginger
5 g dried red chilli
2 finely sliced large onions
1 pinch monosodium gluto-
     mate (ajinomoto)
1 pinch bicarbonate of soda
     oil for frying
     seasoning

Method

Prepare the brèdes, depending on variety used.
Crush the garlic and ginger together and add the chilli.
Heat the oil in a pan on a moderate heat.
Fry the onions in the oil for one minute. Do not colour.
Add the crushed garlic and root ginger.
Add the brèdes and fry until cooked.
Sprinkle the bicarbonate of soda over the leaves and stir.
Season to taste, adding the monosodium glutomate.
Chopped bacon may also be added if desired.
This dish is usually served with Creole rice and various chutneys.
For a change, salt fish may be added to the brèdes.

Chou chou may also be used for this dish.
Cook the chou chou in boiling water.
Cut in half and remove the stone.
Slice and with a fork make a purée with the chou chou.
Then proceed as for the brèdes.

Note:
In this dish, the leaves of different vegetables can be used — the leaves of chou chou, the malabar plant, pumpkin or drumstick. In each case use only the small tender leaves. If you use the leaves of Chinese cabbage, white cabbage, radish or beetroot, shred them finely before cooking.

Creole Rice

Ingredients

1 kg Basmati rice
1¼ litres water
    seasoning

Method

Wash the rice several times in running water.
Place the rice in a pan with the water and season.
Place a lid on the pan.
Bring to the boil on a fast heat.
When the rice is cooked, put the pot to one side of the stove on a very low heat.
The rice will continue to cook and will dry slowly.
Allow approximately forty-five minutes for cooking.

The popular commercial version of Creole rice is as follows:

Ingredients

1   kg Basmati rice
1¼ litres water
50   g saffron
2   red pimentos
2   sweet green peppers
1   tablespoon garden peas
100 g sliced mushrooms
1   large onion
10   g chopped parsley
6   tomatoes
       oil for frying

Method

Cook the rice exactly as for Creole rice.
When the rice is cooked, fold in the saffron.
Slice the red pimentos and green peppers finely.
Chop the onion roughly, and cut the tomatoes into six.
Heat the oil in a pan.
Fry the chopped onion for one minute. Do not colour.
Add the rest of the ingredients to the onion.
Fry gently for about one minute.
Fold all these ingredients into the rice.
Basmati rice is the best rice for the dish because it has more flavour.

Sweet Corn Fritters

Ingredients

1   egg
1   tin sweet corn niblets
2   celery stalks
1   sweet green pepper
60 g raw prawns
1   fresh green chilli
6   spring onions
60 g flour
10 g baking powder
    seasoning
    oil for deep frying

Method

Clean the spring onions, green peppers and celery.
Take the onions, peppers and chilli and grind to a paste.
Clean the prawns and chop finely.
Dice the celery finely and add sweet corn.
Place all the above ingredients in a bowl.
Break the egg into the mixture and stir.
Add the flour, baking powder and seasoning.
Stir well to form a smooth batter.
Place the oil in a deep pan.
Bring the oil to smoking point, turn to a lower heat.
Drop in large spoonfuls of the batter.
Deep fry until a golden brown, turning when necessary.
Drain well. Serve hot with chilli sauce (page 28).

Fried Aubergines

Ingredients

2 medium aubergines
5 chopped spring onions
5 g grated root ginger
2 finely chopped green
  chillies
3 crushed black cardamoms
8 cloves crushed garlic
5 g crushed fennel
1 cinnamon stick
1 cup coconut milk
  (page 79)
½ cup curry paste
  seasoning
  oil for frying

Method

Slice the aubergines lengthways into four.
Cut from base to stem leaving stem intact.
Sprinkle with salt, and leave for five minutes.
(This draws the bitter juices from the aubergines.)
Rinse and dry the aubergines after five minutes.
Heat 5 cm of oil and fry the aubergines until soft.
Drain and cool after cooking.
Place a little of the oil in a pan and fry the onions
and garlic for one minute.
Add rest of the ingredients with the exception of the
coconut milk.
Cook for a further four minutes on a moderate heat,
stirring frequently.
Pour in the coconut milk and blend into the paste.
Season.
Return aubergines to the mix and heat.
Serve hot or cold as a main dish or side dish.

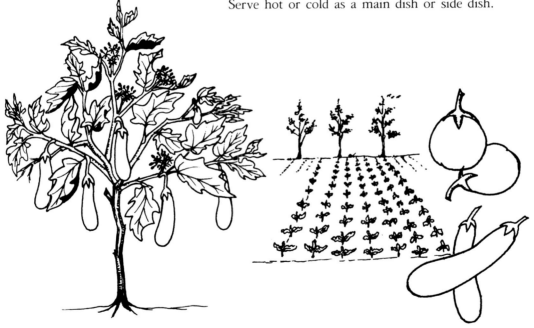

Fricassée of Corn Fish

Ingredients

1   corn fish
2   chillies cut in half
1   sprig parsley
1   clove crushed garlic
10 g crushed root ginger
1   cinnamon stick
1   coarsely chopped onion
1   sprig fresh thyme
3   crushed cloves
2   cups dry white wine
1   bay leaf
3   whole peeled tomatoes
    juice of one lemon
    oil for frying
    seasoning

Method

Cut the head and tail off and remove the skin from the fish.
Cut into bite size pieces and wash under running water.
Place the oil in a pan to heat.
Fry the onions, garlic and ginger for thirty seconds.
Add the fish and fry both sides for two minutes.
Pour in the white wine and simmer for one minute.
Cut the tomatoes in half.
Add the rest of the ingredients to the fish.
Cook until the fish is tender and falls off the bone.
Remove the thyme, cinnamon and parsley.
Season to taste.
Serve with Creole rice (page 25).

Bouillon of Tec Tec

Ingredients

500 g tec tec
2   coarsely cut onions
3   cloves crushed garlic
15   g crushed root ginger
2   crushed chillies
2   bay leaves
1   sprig fresh thyme
1   sprig parsley
2   whole peeled tomatoes
     oil for frying
     seasoning

Method

For the stock half water and half rice water (water which has had rice cooked in it) should be used.
Boil the tec tec in the above stock for ten minutes.
Place the oil in a pan to heat.
Fry the onions until soft.
Add the rest of the ingredients.
Cook for two minutes.
Strain the tec tec stock into the onions, etc.
Cook for a further ten minutes.
Strain through a fine muslin.
Season to taste.

Crab Jhislaine

Ingredients

4 large crabs
1 finely chopped onion
2 cloves crushed garlic
1 sprig fresh thyme
1 bay leaf
1 crushed chilli
1 pinch paprika
  juice of one lemon
  oil for frying
  seasoning

Method

Clean the crab and remove the meat from the shell.
Cut the flesh into bite size pieces.
Place the oil in a pan and heat.
Put the crab into the heated oil and cook for three minutes.
Pour over just sufficient water to cover the crab meat.
Add the rest of the ingredients and stir in.
Cook for five minutes or until the water evaporates.
Remove the sprig of thyme and bay leaf.
Replace the cooked crab into the cleaned crab shell.
Serve instantly with Creole rice (page 25) and chevrette chutney (page 74), coconut chutney (page 76) or Dominique chutney (page 75).

Mauritian Style Pasta

Ingredients

500 g spaghetti or macaroni
1   litre milk
4   egg yolks
250 g butter
250 g grated cheddar cheese
1   sprig fresh thyme
10   g chopped parsley
250 g crushed cream
       crackers
2   sliced tomatoes
1   finely chopped onion
1   clove crushed garlic
1   crushed chilli
     oil for frying
     seasoning

Method

Boil the spaghetti or macaroni in water with a little salt.
When cooked, but not too soft, remove from the water.
Place the oil in a pan and heat.
Fry the onions, chilli, thyme and the garlic together until soft, but not brown.
Add the cooked macaroni or spaghetti and mix it in.
Add some butter and cheese and let the mixture cook for a few minutes.
Pour in the milk and the eggs beaten together.
Stir well into the macaroni mix.
Season to taste and remove the sprig of thyme.
Place the macaroni into a casserole dish.
Sprinkle the crushed biscuits and small pieces of butter on top of the macaroni.
Place the sliced tomatoes on top and brown the surface under a hot grill.
Instead of milk chopped corned beef can be added to the macaroni.

Red Mullet with Palm Heart

Ingredients

4   red mullet (filleted)
3   tomatoes
1   crushed chilli
1   bay leaf
1   heart of palm
1   finely chopped onion
1   sprig fresh thyme
100 g butter
      juice of one lemon
      milk
      seasoning

Method

Cook the heart of palm for fifteen minutes in the milk.
When the palm is cooked, remove from the milk.
Cut into four and place three pieces into the liquidizer.
Liquidize the palm heart into a purée and then strain.
Keep the juice on one side.
Chop the fourth piece of palm into pieces.
Place the palm juice into a casserole dish.
Cut the tomatoes in half and remove the seeds.
Cut the flesh into six.
Place all the ingredients into the casserole.
Lay the fish fillets on top of the ingredients.
Season.
Cover with foil and cook for ten minutes.
When cooked remove the fish from the liquor.
Serve the garnish over the fish with a little of the liquor.

Octopus Daube

Ingredients

1   kg cleaned octopus
500 g whole peeled tomatoes
15   g fresh coriander
2   cups red wine
15   g chopped parsley
1   chopped onion
5   crushed cloves
1   sprig fresh thyme
15   g crushed root ginger
2   cloves crushed garlic
3   chillies cut into four
     oil for frying
     seasoning

Method

Cut the octopus into bite size pieces.
Place the wine and 1 litre of water in pan.
Add the octopus to the liquid and boil for fifteen minutes.
Place oil into pan and heat.
Fry the onions and garlic for thirty seconds.
Add the rest of the ingredients, except the tomatoes, and cook for one minute.
Cut the tomatoes in half and add to the above.
When the octopus is cooked add to the tomatoes, etc.
Cook for a further three minutes, adding octopus stock if required.
The daube should finish red in colour and with a rich sauce.
Remove the coriander and thyme before serving.
Calamary may be used instead of octopus.

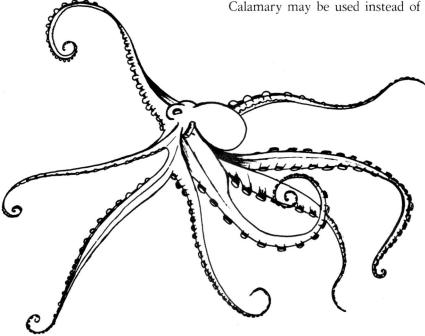

Touffé Ricon

Ingredients

6   pieces of ricon fish
250 g tomatoes
5   g of ginger
1   cleaned onion
3   cloves garlic
4   whole big onions
1   branch of parsley leaves
        (optional)
1   lemon
     ajinomoto (to taste)
     oil for frying
     seasoning

Method

Clean, wash and cut the fish.
Season with ground pepper and salt to taste, then half fry the fish.
Cut the onions.
Grind the garlic and ginger on the roche carri.
Place the oil into a pan and heat.
Fry the ground garlic and ginger for one minute and add the onions.
Put in the tomatoes and parsley.
Allow the mixture to cook for five minutes.
Add the half fried fish and mix with ½ cup of water.
Allow to cook for ten minutes on a low flame.
Season to taste.

Black Pudding Omelette

Ingredients

3   eggs
1   tablespoon fresh cream
5   g chopped parsley
5   g chopped thyme
60 g finely diced black
    pudding
15 g finely chopped onion
    oil for frying
    seasoning

Method

Break the eggs into a bowl with a little seasoning.
Beat well, adding the herbs and the cream.
Heat the oil in a pan.
Fry the onions for thirty seconds.
Add the black pudding and cook for a further thirty
seconds.
Add the eggs to the pan and mix well together.
Proceed as for a normal omelette.

Bread Fruit Croquettes

Ingredients

500 g bread fruit
1   egg
25 g butter
1   finely chopped onion
1   pinch nutmeg
2   teaspoons milk
    cornflour
    oil for frying
    seasoning

Method

Remove the skin from the bread fruit.
Cut into pieces and boil in salted water.
When cooked remove from the water.
Crush the bread fruit to a purée.
Heat the oil in a pan.
Fry the onions in the oil until soft.
Add the onions to the bread fruit.
Season to taste and stir in the milk and nutmeg.
Add a little cornflour to the paste to make it firm.
Make the paste into small balls.
Fry in hot oil.
Serve hot.

Fricassée of Haricots Rouges

Ingredients

1	kg haricots rouges
250	g pork fat
4	chillies cut into four
15	g parsley sprigs
1	sprig fresh thyme
3	cloves crushed garlic
1	cinammon stick
10	crushed cloves
250	g whole peeled tomatoes
2	coarsely chopped onions
2	bay leaves
15	g crushed root ginger
	oil for frying
	salt

Method

Soak the beans in water overnight.
In the morning strain the beans from the water.
Place the pork fat into a pan of clean water.
Bring to the boil and add the beans with a little salt.
Cook for approximately twenty minutes.
Place the oil into a pan and heat.
Fry the onions, garlic, thyme and ginger for thirty seconds.
Add the rest of the ingredients and cook for three minutes.
When cooked, strain the beans from the water.
Add the beans to the fricassée mix and cook for five minutes.
Remove bay leaf, thyme and parsley.
Serve with Creole rice (page 25) and chevrette chutney (page 74).

Pawpaw Belle Mare

Ingredients

2   pawpaw
2   cleaned celery sticks
1   crushed chilli
2   spring onions
180 g grated cheddar cheese
30   g butter
30   g flour
½   litre milk
1   pinch nutmeg
     seasoning

Method

Peel the pawpaw and remove the seeds.
Place a pan of salted water on to boil.
Chop the spring onion and celery and pawpaw.
Place the chopped ingredients into the boiling water.
Cook until tender.
Drain off the water.
Put the milk on to boil.
Mix the flour and butter together to a soft paste.
Whisk this into the milk and cook until the sauce thickens.
Add the cooked pawpaw, chilli and vegetables to the sauce.
Place the mixture into a dish. Sprinkle with nutmeg.
Place the cheese on top and brown in a hot oven (200°C).

Quatre Quatre Manioc

Ingredients

1   chilli cut in half
1   kg manioc
3   tomatoes
10   g crushed root ginger
1   clove crushed garlic
1   onion finely chopped
15   g chopped parsley
250   g pork fat
     oil for frying
     seasoning

Method

Peel and wash the manioc. Cut it into four or five pieces.
Boil it in the water, with a little salt, until cooked but not too soft.
When cooked remove the manioc from the water.
Place the oil in a pan and heat.
Fry the onions, pork fat and garlic together for one minute.
Cut the tomatoes in half and add to the above.
Add a little water and then the rest of the ingredients.
Cover with a lid and cook for three minutes.
Season to taste.
Serve with Creole rice (page 25).

Repas Créole

Nous pêcherons pour vous complaire
Dans les roches de la rivière
Ecrevisse à notre manière.
        Le Camaron.

Nous abattrons dans la ravine
Sans respect de sa fière mine
Pour son coeur à la chair si fine
        Le Chou-palmiste.

Nous servirons en bonne aubaine
Dans un grand bol de porcelaine
Du riz de Chine ou bier de l'Inde
        Aux grains laiteux.

Agrémentant cette blancheur
Sous le parfum et la couleur
Nous dispenserons sa saveur
        Poule au carri.

Complément de notre ripaille
Flanquant le carri de volaille
Les pommes d'amour en rougaille
        Seront en fleurs.

Pour corser de facon experte
Le piquant de l'agape offerte
Nous hacherons la mangue verte
        En chatini.

La gamme des feux du tropique
Exprimera sa politique
Par ces représentants toniques,
        Piments, achards.

Constitueront notre réserve
Pour que chaque jour on les serve
Modérateurs de notre verve,
        Bouillons de brèdes.

Atte, bibasse, bigarade,
Letchis à pulpe délectable,
Le verger sera sur la table,
        Exquis déssert.

Rhums de chez nous et vins de France,
Cafés de chaude succulence
Complèteront avec science
        Notre régal.

Chère, laissant votre auréole,
Par le prochain 'zinc' qui décolle
Venez ce soir à la créole
        Dîner aux Iles.

Clément Charoux

Indian Cooking

nice and spicy

The Indians who began arriving in Mauritius in the early nineteenth century came mainly from the state of Bihar in India but also from towns and villages scattered in the areas around Madras and Bombay. The type of cooking they brought to this island therefore cannot be associated with a specific regional variety of Indian cuisine. However, those elements basic to all Indian cooking — rice, flour, dholl and ghee — were imported into Mauritius on a large scale only with the arrival of the Indian worker.

In the slave days, the staple diet had been cassava or *manioc* — a fleshy root originally introduced by Mahé de Labourdonnais. Now rice became the standard article of food. It still is. In Indian cooking long-grained rice is preferred. Patna and Basmati are the best-known types. Kinds of flour range from wholewheat and lentil or gram flour to white wheat flour. Dholl or *dhall* are dried beans and peas, and ghee is clarified butter. Ghee is used to fry sweet and savoury foods, and is as central to Indian cuisine as soya sauce is to Chinese. The use of ghee often accounts for the rich, nutty flavour of Indian cooking. Ghee can be purchased in packets or tins.

The curry is of course the most famous of Indian dishes, almost as international as spaghetti and hamburgers. Currying is the process of adding crushed spices to meat, fish, seafoods and vegetables. The particular spices chosen and the proportions in which they mix and mingle produce a vast set of permutations, an infinite variety.

In countries like Mauritius where curries are a regular feature of the daily menu, fresh spices are crushed every day on a flat rock (*roche carri*) placed in the backyard for that purpose. Each spice or herb is ground with a cylindrical stone called a *baba*, which is like an oversized, petrified rolling pin. When the mixture of all the crushed ingredients becomes a paste it is ready to be added to the fried onions and tomatoes. Commercial curry powder is a dehydrated version of that paste.

Dried saffron and coriander seeds are at the basis of any paste of spices. Saffron not only gives a delicate flavouring but also that flash of yellow-orange so evocative of the East. Coriander, known locally as *cotomili*, is used both as grains and as leaves. In Chinese cuisine the leaves are referred to as Chinese parsley. In addition to saffron and coriander seeds a standard Mauritian curry paste will consist of crushed ginger, garlic and dried red chillies or fresh green ones.

1. *Dried chillies (piments secs).*
2. *Cinnamon (cannelle).*
3. *Saffron (turmeric).*
4. *Root ginger.*
5. *Carri poulet.*
6. *Garlic (ail).*
7. *Cloves (girofle).*
8. *Caraway (small) (tilani).*
9. *Black pepper.*
10. *Metti.*
11. *Coriander seeds.*
12. *Mustard seeds.*
13. *Anis seeds (big).*

Chillies grow well in the north of the island, and come in three varieties — *ti piment* (small), *gros piment* (large), and *piment carri* — the last being a misnomer since it is very mild, usually fried in batter, and eaten as a snack rather than in curries. The small variety of chilli used in curries, or nibbled whole after being soaked in brine and then oil, is powerful enough to make human hair curl. The large variety, in comparison, is considerably kinder on the taste buds. It is often chopped up and used in salads, like green peppers. The dried red chillies come from India.

Other ingredients that you will come across in our recipes are tamarind, cumin seed, cardamom, cinnamom and curry leaves. Tamarind trees are found mainly on the hot, dry west coast of Mauritius. There is even a small fishing village in the area which bears the name. The trees bear long green pods, like huge beans. These turn brown and brittle as they ripen. When the outer shell is cracked, the dark, sticky brown flesh is revealed. It is more sour than sweet. Mauritian school children eat it dipped in crude salt, and housewives boil it with water to make a *compote* and a tangy drink. The name tamarind means 'Indian date' in Persian.

Cardamom is known in Mauritius as *laïti*, which comes from the Indian *elaichi*; cinnamom is known as *kanel* from the French *canelle*; caraway is called *tilani* because it is related to the *anis*. Thus the Mauritian synthesis of cuisines brings together not only ingredients from the four continents, but also their appellations from languages as unrelated as French and Hindi.

The term *carri poulet*, used to refer to curry leaves, seems to be an indigenous invention. The French call them *feuilles à carri* and the Indians *khadi patta*. Since chicken curry is a Mauritian favourite, this might account for the appearance of 'poulet' in the name. Curry leaves are from a small shrub of the orange family. They have a unique fragrance which makes their presence in a respectable curry indispensable. Bay leaves offer a totally different flavour and are therefore a poor substitute.

Curries are eaten with rice or *faratas* (Indian bread), and accompanied by a variety of chutneys and *achards*. Recipes for these form an important part of this section. Chutneys or *chatinis* are the solid equivalent of the tropical cocktail. A number of contrasting goodies are thrown together to produce a concoction which is both powerful and pretty, but which must be relished in small quantities. Our selection includes the typical *chatini pomme d'amour* together with the less conventional fresh mint and crunchy peanut chutnies. The *achard* is a fruit or vegetable pickle. Though the term has come down to us from Persia via India, the dish itself is fairly typical of this part of the world. *Larousse Gastronomique* describes it as being greatly valued 'in the whole Indian Archipelago, in Mauritius and Réunion Island'. The Mauritian *achard* represents one of those grey areas in which Indian and Creole cooking have merged. Distinctions become difficult and, in the final analysis, unnecessary.

Achard is one of those delights that Mauritians living or studying abroad long for, and many an airborne suitcase heading for Europe or Australia is filled with ample jars of the precious substance. Rumour has it that an official letter sent to Her Majesty the Queen was returned because it bore, in addition to the address, a large yellow stain. Officials identified it with a mere sniff as mixed vegetable *achard*. The recipe for it is on page 71.

Indian cooking requires various-sized metal saucepans known as *dekchees*. They have flat lids and no handles. A *karahi*, similar to a Chinese wok, is used in deep frying. *Faratas* are made in a curved iron griddle known as a *tawa*. Food is cooked on low kerosene or charcoal stoves, with the cook sitting on a tiny stool a foot off the ground. In Mauritian villages, firewood collected from the forests is a favourite fuel. The smell of wood smoke, of browning *faratas* and pungent curries are as part of our twilight atmosphere as the setting sun itself.

Gâteau Piment

Ingredients

½ kg dholl
2 fresh chillies
4 spring onions
1 pinch salt
10 g anis (caraway seeds) or
    soja
1 pinch saffron powder
1 egg
1 sprig freshly chopped
    coriander leaves
    oil for frying

Method

Wash and clean the dholl thoroughly.
Put the dholl into 125 ml of water and boil for five minutes.
Strain the dholl and place on a cloth to dry.
Crush the anis or, if using soja, chop finely.
Put the dholl on to a roche carri and crush.
Chop the chillies and spring onions very finely.
Add all the ingredients to the crushed dholl.
Mix in thoroughly for even distribution.
Heat the oil in a pan until very hot.
Make small balls with the paste and drop them into the fat carefully.
Fry until crisp and golden brown outside.
Eat hot.

Samoosa

Ingredients

280 g minced beef
1   minced onion
2   cloves minced garlic
15   g minced ginger root
5   g finely chopped
     coriander leaves
45   g ghee
5   g turmeric
5   g mustard seeds
5   minced chillies
20   g curry powder
     juice of one lemon
     seasoning
     oil for frying

Method

For the wrappers of the samoosa use the spring roll recipe on page 82.

Cook the beef in a little water until no moisture is left.

Fry the onion and garlic in the ghee. Do not colour.

Add the ginger and the cooked meat to the onion.

Cook for two minutes.

Add the remaining ingredients and heat thoroughly.

Having cut the pastry into circles of 15 cm across, place the circles on to a heated *tawa*.

Heat both sides of the pastry for ten seconds.

Remove from *tawa* and place on to a floured board.

Cut each circle into triangles.

Fold ends over to form a triangular pocket.

Fill the pocket with the samoosa mixture.

Fold corner over to get a triangular shape.

Stick ends down with a little cold water.

Deep fry the samoosa until golden brown.

Serve hot with mint or peanut chutney.

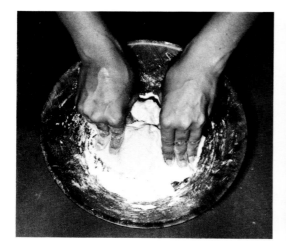
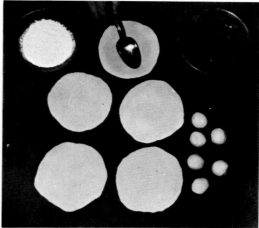

Dholl Puri

Ingredients

1 kg dholl
1 kg flour
1 pinch saffron

Method

Wash and clean the dholl thoroughly.
Cook the dholl in 125 ml water for eight minutes.
Strain the dholl and allow to cool in a container.
Keep the dholl water.
Place the flour on to a table and form a well in the centre.
Pour the dholl water slowly into the flour.
Form a smooth paste.
Knead for a good eight minutes until the dough becomes soft and supple.
Put the paste into a bowl and cover.
Allow to stand for half an hour.
Oil your hands and take sufficient paste to form a medium sized ball.
Cut the ball open and place some dholl inside.
Roll the ball in the palm of your hands to close it again.
Place the ball of paste on to a board and roll into a circle of 20 cm diameter.
From this point cook as for faratas (page 55).

Faratas

Ingredients

2   kg flour
125 ml oil
250 ml warm water
1   pinch salt

Method

Place the flour and salt on to a table and make a well.
Add the water little by little.
Mix the water into the flour with your hands to form
a smooth dough.
Oil your hands to prevent dough from sticking to
your fingers.
Pour the oil over the dough and knead well for ten
minutes until the dough becomes soft and smooth.
Place in a bowl and cover with a cloth.
Let the pastry rest for at least half an hour.
Take small balls from the dough.
Roll them out into circles about 20 cm in diameter.
Brush a little oil on the top of each pastry circle.
Turn the pastry over and brush the other side with oil.
To fold the pastry into sections, take the outside of
the circle and fold to the centre of the circle.
Repeat this with the other side of the circle to meet
the first fold.
Turn the pastry over and fold again as above.
This operation will leave you with a folded square.
Do this until all the dough is used up. Cover with a cloth.
Heat pan on a low heat.
Brush the pan with a very little oil.
Roll the folded square paste into a round again.
Shape and place in the pan.
Cook for half a minute and turn it over to cook other
side.
Whilst the second side is cooking brush the top with oil.
Cook for a further half a minute and turn farata over
again.
Brush with oil and repeat the turning over and oiling
until the farata is cooked.
The farata is used mainly by the Indian community
who eat it instead of rice. It is served with a variety
of foods, eg dholl, pumpkin, fricassée, brèdes songe
and various chutneys.
The farata is then broken into pieces with the fingers
and used to scoop up the food.
Knives and forks are not usually used.
If any faratas are left over, these are often eaten with
butter the next day for breakfast.

Mulligatawny Soup

Ingredients

1   kg cleaned chicken
1   litre chicken stock
2   large cleaned onions
8   cloves garlic
10   g ground cumin
10   g turmeric powder
3   black cardamoms
1   cinnamon stick
10   coriander leaves
20   g ghee or oil
3   chillies
3   bay leaves
1   cup coconut milk
     (page 79)
30   g butter
20   g flour
30   g cooked rice
5   g saffron
     seasoning

Method

Chop the onion finely.

Cook the chicken in the chicken stock with the onions.

Crush the garlic and chillies with a little salt.

Place the oil or ghee in pan on a moderate heat and cook the garlic and chillies for one minute in it.

Add the rest of the spices and cook for a further two minutes.

Combine this with the chicken and stock and continue cooking.

When the chicken is tender remove from the stock.

Remove the meat from the chicken and cut into fine dice.

Make a paste with the flour and butter.

Blend this into the soup and mix well.

Whisk or stir well to prevent any lumps from forming. It will now be of a thicker consistency.

Remove the coriander and bay leaves.

Season to taste.

Add the chicken meat, coconut milk and rice to the soup.

Serve in a tureen.

Raçon (Rassam)

Ingredients

1   kg songe
5   g saffron powder
5   g black peppercorns
4   green chillies
5   cloves garlic
2   g root ginger
5   g aniseed
2   onions
10 g tamarind
5   curry leaves
2   peeled tomatoes
    oil for frying
    water
    seasoning

Method

Boil the songe in water for approximately twelve minutes.

Soak the tamarind in cold water for ten minutes to dissolve.

Liquidize or crush the garlic, ginger, aniseed and peppercorns.

When the songe is cooked, strain and keep the water.

Clean and chop the onions and curry leaves.

Cut the tomatoes and chillies into julienne.

Heat the oil in the pan.

Place the liquidized ingredients into the oil.

Add the onions, curry leaves, tomatoes, saffron and chillies.

Strain the tamarind and songe water into the mixture.

Cook for twenty minutes. Remove the curry leaves.

Prior to serving cut half the cooked songe into a very fine dice and add to the raçon.

Season to taste.

If green chillies are not available use dried chillies.

These can be added to the bouillon at the last minute.

Note:
This dish is a typically 'Madras' dish, though less hot. For extra 'fire' a tot of rum may be added to the raçon just prior to serving.

Fish Curry à la Madras

Ingredients

5   fish fillets
1   large onion chopped
25   g grated root ginger
10   cloves crushed garlic
3   chopped spring onions
5   g crushed fenugreek
100   g curry powder
20   g saffron
75   g tamarind
3   aubergines
2   green chopped chillies
10   coriander leaves
3   peeled tomatoes
250   ml water
1   sprig fresh thyme
5   curry leaves
      oil for frying.

Method

Cut fish into required size.
Cut the aubergines lengthways into four.
Mix the curry powder and saffron together.
Cut the tomatoes into julienne.
Add the tamarind to the water to dissolve.
Heat the oil in a pan on a moderate fire.
Add the onions to the oil and fry but do not colour.
Add the ginger, garlic, saffron and curry mix to the onions.
Let this cook for three minutes over a slow fire.
Add the tomatoes.
Strain the tamarind water into the curry mixture. Stir well.
Add the fish, aubergines, thyme, curry and coriander leaves, chillies, fenugreek and sprig of thyme.
Place lid on pan and cook slowly for eight minutes, or until the fish is cooked.
Remove curry and coriander leaves and thyme sprig before serving and add the chopped spring onions.
The best chutneys to serve with this dish are crushed tomato and lemon achard (page 73 and 72).

Note:
The best fish for this dish are sacréchien, mullet or capitaine. The aubergines used are the long baby ones. Again this is a typical 'Madras' dish. Note the use of tamarind which is one of the most popular items to serve with songe.

Goat Curry

Ingredients

	heart, lungs, liver and tripe of a goat
1	litre of goat's blood
1	large chopped onion
25	g grated root ginger
5	cloves crushed garlic
15	curry leaves
1	sprig fresh thyme
4	sliced tomatoes
5	chopped spring onions
100	g curry powder
15	fresh coriander leaves
3	chopped green chillies
25	g saffron
	oil for frying

Method

Cut the innards of the goat into pieces.
Place a pan of water on to boil. Season.
Wash and clean the tripe and cut into bite size pieces.
Place the tripe into the water for two minutes to blanch.
Remove the tripe and add to the rest of the goat's offal.
Proceed exactly as for chicken curry (page 60).
When nearly cooked add the pieces of thickened blood.
Cook until meat is tender.
Serve with Creole rice (page 25) and various chutneys (pages 71 to 76).

Note:
When the goat is killed the blood is kept in a container and used for this dish. Salt is added to the blood to thicken it. The blood is then cut into small cubes and added to the curry.

Chicken Curry

Ingredients

750 g boned chicken
1   large chopped onion
25   g grated root ginger
5   cloves crushed garlic
15   curry leaves
4   fresh sliced tomatoes
1   sprig thyme
5   chopped spring onions
100 g curry powder
16   fresh coriander leaves
3   chopped green chillies
2   peeled potatoes
2   tablespoons garden peas
¼   litre chicken stock
⅙   litre cooking oil
25   g saffron

Method

Cut the meat into 30 g cubes.
Cut the potato into small cubes.
Heat the oil in a pan on a moderate heat and cook the chicken.
Remove the meat and keep to one side.
Add onion, ginger, garlic, curry powder and saffron to the remaining oil.
Allow to cook on a slow heat for two or three minutes.
Stir continuously so as not to burn.
Add thyme, coriander, spring onions and chillies all finely chopped.
Stir in the curry mix.
Add the meat and curry leaves and thoroughly mix into the curry mixture.
Add chicken stock and potatoes. Stir well.
Cover the pan with a lid and cook until the potatoes are ready.
Finally add tomatoes and peas and heat.
Take out the curry leaves, coriander leaves and thyme.
The curry sauce must not taste grainy. If it does it needs more cooking.
Season to taste.
Serve with Creole rice (page 25), papadums and various chutneys (pages 71 to 76).

Chicken Tika

Ingredients

1kg 200g chicken
100 g tomatoes
2   teaspoons chilli sauce (page 28)
2   cloves crushed garlic
10   g crushed root ginger
3   g paprika
1   pkt white breadcrumbs
     oil for frying
     seasoning

For the batter

250 g flour
2   eggs
2   drops yellow colouring
     water

Method

Remove all the meat from the bones of the chicken.
Cut the meat into small dice.
Peel and chop the tomatoes very finely.
Add all the ingredients together, with the exception of
the breadcrumbs.
Mix well together.
Season to taste.
Refrigerate for one hour.

For the batter, whisk the ingredients together to form
a smooth paste.
Ensure that the batter is not too thick but is of a
creamy consistency.
Remove the chicken mix from the refrigerator.
Press together and thread on to brochette sticks.
Roll the chicken brochettes into the white
breadcrumbs.
Dip into the batter and deep fry until golden brown.
Serve with Creole sauce (page 29) and various achards
(pages 71 and 72).

Dholl Curry

Ingredients

250 g dholl
1   large cleaned onion
5   g crushed root ginger
5   cloves crushed garlic
1   sprig fresh thyme
8   curry leaves
10   fresh coriander leaves
3   peeled tomatoes
50   g curry powder
20   g saffron
4   chopped spring onions
½   litre chicken stock
2   chopped chillies
     oil for frying

Method

Wash and clean the dholl.
Cook in water until of a smooth purée consistency.
Chop the cleaned onion.
Heat oil in a pan on a moderate heat.
Fry the onions in the oil. Do not colour.
Add the garlic and ginger.
Combine the curry and saffron powder and mix well.
Cook on a slow heat, stirring well so as not to burn.
Chop the tomatoes into eight pieces and add to the curry mix.
Add the thyme, chillies, spring onions, curry leaves and coriander leaves.
Pour in ½ the stock and allow the curry to cook for three minutes.
When the dholl is cooked add the rest of the stock.
Stir in well, adding the curry mix at the same time.
Remove the coriander, thyme and curry leaves.
The consistency of the curry should be that of a thickish sauce.
The amount of stock required can vary, so either add more stock or use less, according to taste.
Serve with salted fish, coconut chutney and Creole rice (pages 29, 76, 25).
Coriander leaves may be chopped finely and sprinkled on top prior to serving.

Dholl Pita

Ingredients

750 g dholl
10 g grated root ginger
6 cloves crushed garlic
8 large onions
6 red chillies
15 g crushed root saffron
30 g ghee
    seasoning to taste
    water

Method

Clean and chop the onions finely.
Melt the ghee in a pan on a moderate heat.
Place the onions in the ghee and fry but do not colour. Remove and keep apart.
Fry the spices in the ghee for one minute.
Wash the dholl several times to clean it.
Add the dholl to the spices and stir well.
Cover the dholl with about 8 cm of hot water.
Place the lid on pan and cook on a moderate heat.
Stir occasionally to prevent burning.
Cook until the dholl becomes a smooth purée consistency and then add the fried onions.

For the paste

500 g flour
    salt
    oil
    water

Make a firm paste with the ingredients.
Take the paste and roll out very thinly.
Cut the paste into squares or fancy shapes.
Drop the pieces into the dholl which is nearly cooked.
Care must be taken not to cook the pastry shapes too much. They should be cooked but not soft.
The dholl should be served neither too thick nor as a soup.
Serve with coconut chutney (page 76), and with chopped coriander leaves sprinkled on top.

Briani

Ingredients

750 g rice
600 g chicken
500 g peeled potatoes
1   tablespoon peas
1   teaspoon saffron flower
250 ml oil
1   large onion
5   g cumin seeds
5   g cardamom seeds
1   cinnamom stick
200 g vegetable margarine
         or ghee
5   g fresh coriander leaf
5   mint leaves
10   g crushed root ginger
5   cloves crushed garlic
1   natural yoghurt
1   teaspoon
         yellow colouring

Method

Cut the chicken into small pieces.
Marinate for one hour in yoghurt and half the quantity of all the spices.
Slice and fry the onion. Add to the marinade.
Cut the potatoes into quarters and cook as roast potatoes until they are just coloured.
Half cook the rice in boiling water.
Drain the rice and dry well.
Mix half the margarine and yellow colour with the rice. Stir until blended together. The rice should be both yellow and white.
Half cook the chicken in oil with the marinade.
Take a large pot and grease well with the remaining margarine.
Place a layer of rice on the bottom of the pot.
Take a few pieces of chicken, potato and peas and place on top of the rice.
Sprinkle a little of the remaining spices and saffron on the top.
On top of chicken, etc place another layer of rice.
Repeat process of layering chicken, spices and rice until all the rice has been used.
Place a lid on the pot and seal with a flour paste so that no steam escapes.
Place in a medium oven for thirty minutes.
Take the pot from oven, remove sealed lid and serve immediately.
Serve with various chutneys.

Chicken Vindaloo

Ingredients

1	kg boned chicken
500	g small potatoes
2	cleaned and finely chopped onions
15	g crushed coriander seeds
100	g curry powder
5	curry leaves
5	g crushed root ginger
1	crushed chilli
4	cloves crushed garlic
3	sliced tomatoes
½	cup natural yoghurt
5	g salt
2	cups water
10	g turmeric
	oil for frying

Method

Cut the chicken into bite size pieces and wash well.
Scrub and boil the potatoes in their jackets until firm but not too soft.
Allow to cool, peel the skin off and cut the potatoes in half.
Mix the onions, garlic, curry leaves, coriander and ginger together. Stir into the curry powder, salt, chilli and yoghurt.
Take half of the onion and curry mixture and add the potatoes to it.
Heat oil in the pan on a moderate heat.
Add the other half of the curry mixture and cook for two minutes. Stir to prevent burning.
Stir in the small pieces of chicken until well cooked.
Let it stand for two hours.
Add the turmeric and tomatoes and heat.
Pour in the water and allow to simmer on a low heat.
Cook until the chicken is tender.
Add the seasoned potatoes carefully, mixing them with the chicken.
If necessary add more water.

Naraisi Kofta

Meat balls with egg inside

Ingredients

400 g finely minced beef
50 g split pea flour
10 g turmeric
½ cup yoghurt
7 eggs
110 g curry powder
5 g salt
1 clove crushed garlic
1 onion finely chopped
1 crushed chilli
1 cup water
   oil for deep frying

Method

Pour the water into a pan with the beef and place on a moderate heat.
Add the garlic, curry powder, turmeric, salt and the chilli.
Bring to the boil and cook on a low heat for fifteen minutes.
Sprinkle the split pea flour on top and stir in.
Cook for a further ten minutes.
When the meat is very soft and dry, mash and knead thoroughly.
Lightly beat one egg.
Mix in the yoghurt and a little of the beaten egg.
Stir in well and knead again.
Hard boil the six eggs. Cool under cold running water and shell.
Take some of the well worked mixture and flatten it in your hand.
Place one of the hard boiled eggs inside the worked mixture.
Wrap the mixture around the egg, covering the egg completely.
Place the oil in a pan on a high heat until it reaches smoking point.
Dip each kofta into the remaining beaten egg.
Fry in the oil on a moderate heat until golden brown.
Drain well and serve.

To curry the koftas use the curry sauce from the chicken curry (page 60) adding sliced green peppers and coriander seeds.

Alu and Varhia

Ingredients

½   kg small potatoes
3   sliced tomatoes
5   g chopped coriander
      leaves
5   g ghee
5   g salt
5   g turmeric
1   onion cleaned and diced
50 g curry powder
1   cup water
100 g yoghurt
1   crushed chilli
5   g crushed root ginger
3   varhia

Method

Place the ghee in a pan on a moderate heat.
Fry the onions, ginger, coriander and varhia until soft
but not brown.
Add the turmeric, chilli and salt. Stir well and cook
for one minute.
Cut the potatoes into quarters and add to the above.
Cook for one minute. Then pour in the water, stirring
all the time.
Allow to cook until the potatoes feel tender but are
not broken.
Add the sliced tomatoes, curry powder and yoghurt.
Let the curry simmer for ten to fifteen minutes.
Serve with rice and any cooked meat.
In the place of varhia 1 cinnamon stick and 8 cloves
may be used.

Bhuma Chicken

Ingredients

750 g boned chicken
3   cloves garlic
10   curry leaves
5   g freshly chopped
        coriander leaves
5   g root ginger
½   cup yoghurt
30   g ghee
3   sliced tomatoes
5   g turmeric
2   crushed chillies
1   finely chopped onion
10   g finely grated coconut
150 g curry powder
        juice of one lemon

Method

Cut the chicken into bite size pieces and wash well.
Crush the ginger, garlic, coriander, curry leaves and
the onions together.
Mix in the turmeric, salt, curry powder and the
chillies.
Melt the ghee on a low heat.
Fry the above mixture in the ghee for three minutes,
stirring all the time.
Add the tomatoes and yoghurt and mix well.
Add the chicken. Stir into the mix and fry for five
minutes.
Put a lid on the pan and cook on a low heat.
Cook until no liquid is left and the chicken is really
tender.
Remove the lid and add the coconut and lemon juice.
Simmer for two minutes.
The chicken should be quite dry and ready to serve.

Note:
Any kind of poultry may be dry-curried like this.

Khorma

Meat cooked in dry curd

Ingredients

400 g beef
10 g salt
1   green pepper
10 g coriander seeds
115 g curry powder
½   cup yoghurt
15 g butter
10 g turmeric
6   cloves garlic
2   tomatoes
10 g grated coconut
2   chillies
10 g grated root ginger
1   cleaned and sliced onion
½   cup thick coconut milk
    (page 79)

Method

Cut the meat into bite size pieces.
Marinate in the yoghurt for thirty minutes.
Place the marinade and the beef in a pan.
Cook the beef slowly with the salt until tender.
When the beef is cooked remove from the pan.
Crush the garlic, ginger, coriander seeds, chilli, and green pepper together.
Place the butter in pan and melt on a slow heat.
Fry the onions in the butter until soft but not brown.
Add the turmeric, curry powder and the coconut.
Fry for two minutes stirring all the time.
Slice the tomatoes. Add these to the pan and heat.
Stir in the crushed garlic, etc and fry for one minute.
When complete add the already prepared meat and mix well.
Simmer for ten minutes adding the coconut milk.
When ready the khorma should be quite dry and of an attractive colour.

Lamb in Coconut Milk

Ingredients

500 g leg of lamb
1   cup thick coconut milk
     (page 79)
5   g cinnamon
5   g coriander seeds
3   g cumin seeds
1   cardamon seed
2   cloves
1   onion
½   chilli
5   g crushed root ginger
2   cloves crushed garlic
5   g turmeric powder
1   tablespoonful vinegar
     oil for frying
     seasoning

Method

Cut the meat into bite size pieces.
Place all the spices into a pan on a low heat.
Fry lightly for two minutes.
Remove from the pan and grind on a roche carri or
liquidize.
Heat the oil in a pan.
Add the meat to the oil and fry.
Mix the vinegar and crushed spices together.
Add half the coconut milk to the spices, mix well.
Pour this mixture into the meat and cook for ten
minutes.
After the ten minutes of cooking add the remainder of
the milk.
Allow to cook until the meat is tender.
Remove the pan from the heat and allow to cool for
thirty minutes.
Serve with Creole rice (page 25).
Garnish with chopped coriander or mint leaves before
serving.

Mixed Vegetable Achard

Ingredients

1   small cauliflower
150 g French beans
150 g carrots
150 g cabbage
5   chillies cut lengthways
10   g mustard seeds
1   teaspoon saffron
1   small onion
10   g root ginger
2   cloves garlic
¼   litre oil

Method

Crush the mustard seeds, onions, ginger, garlic and saffron together.
Cut the cauliflower into fleurettes.
Cut the cabbage, carrots and French beans finely.
Blanch all the vegetables in boiling water — they must still be crunchy to eat.
Drain the excess water from the vegetables.
Mix the vegetables with the mustard seed mixture and oil.
Add the chillies.
Serve cold as a side dish to any curry.

Mango Achard

Ingredients

10 g mustard seeds
5   g saffron
3   red chillies
¼   litre oil
10 green mangoes
10 g salt

Method

Peel and cut the mangoes into eight pieces.
Add salt and marinate for two hours in the sun.
Crush or liquidize all other ingredients.
Mix with oil.
Add the mangoes to the mixture and blend in.

Note:
Using exactly the same method one can use fruits de cythre, fresh whole green olives and bilimbie.

Achard of Palm Heart

Ingredients

1   palm heart
10 g mustard seeds
5   g saffron
3   red chillies
¼   litre oil
1   litre milk

Method

Cook the palm heart in the milk.
When cooked, remove from milk and drain off excess
liquid.
Crush or liquidize remaining ingredients.
Add to the oil.
Chop the palm heart into cubes.
Add to the above mixture.

Lemon or Orange Achard

Ingredients

10 g mustard seeds
4   g saffron
3   fresh red chillies
¼   litre oil
    peel of 10 lemons
      or oranges

Method

Soak the peel in boiling water for three minutes.
Ensure that no white pith is left on the peel,
otherwise the taste will be bitter.
Cut peel into cubes or julienne.
Leave to dry for one day in the sun or one hour in a
warm oven.
Crush or liquidize the mustard seeds, saffron and
chillies and mix with the oil.
Add the dried lemon peel to the above mixture.
Allow to marinate for a few days before using.

Peanut Chutney

Ingredients

250 g roasted peanuts
3   red chillies
10 mint leaves
4   coriander leaves
    seasoning

Method

Place all the items together in a liquidizer and
grind together until a paste is formed.

Tomato Chutney

Ingredients

2 tomatoes
1 medium onion
3 green chillies
2 fresh mint leaves
  seasoning

Method

Cut the tomatoes into fine strips.
Slice the onion thinly.
Chop the mint leaves and chillies.
Mix all ingredients together.
Season to taste.

Crushed Tomato Chutney

Ingredients

6 peeled tomatoes
1 cleaned onion
3 green chillies
10 fresh coriander leaves
   seasoning

Method

Crush all the ingredients very finely.
Season to taste.

This chutney is very often served with mine or Chinese noodles (page 91).

Brinjal or Aubergine Chutney

Ingredients

6 aubergines
1 onion
2 tomatoes
3 green chillies
1 small cup vinegar
   oil for frying

Method

Deep fry the aubergines whole and remove the skin.
Clean and slice the onion finely.
Liquidize or crush the flesh of the aubergines and chillies.
Heat the oil in a pan.
Fry the onion in the oil until soft but not brown.
Take skin off the tomatoes and cut into half, removing all the pips.
Cut into very fine strips.
Add the onion to the aubergine mix.
Add the tomatoes and vinegar. Mix in well.
Season to taste.

Chevrette Chutney

Ingredients

250 g chevrettes
3   red chillies
2   cloves garlic
5   g ginger
5   peeled tomatoes
     oil for frying

Method

Wash and clean the chevrettes.
Place all the ingredients in a liquidizer or crush.
Heat in oil for two minutes on a slow fire.
Season to taste.

Note:
Chevrettes are shrimps found in Mauritian streams. They are very small and increasingly difficult to find. This is an especially delicious chutney.

Fresh Mint Chutney

Ingredients

100 g fresh mint
1   large onion
2   green chillies
2   teaspoons sugar
    juice of 1 lemon
    salt

Method

Wash the mint and remove the leaves.
Remove the seeds from the chillies.
Crush the onion and chillies together with the salt.
Chop the mint leaves very finely.
Add all the ingredients together and crush to a smooth paste.
Serve with samoosas (page 52).

Coriander Chutney

(Dominique)

Ingredients

120 g coriander leaves
1   teaspoon salt
3   cloves garlic
10 g root ginger
2   teaspoons sugar
    juice of 2 limes

Method

Proceed as for mint chutney.
The final product will become a paste after grinding.

Cooked Peanut Chutney

Ingredients

250 g roasted peanuts
5   peeled tomatoes
4   red chillies
2   onions
1   clove garlic
    oil for frying
    seasoning

Method

Clean and chop the onions finely.
Crush the tomatoes, chillies, garlic and peanuts.
Heat the oil in a pan on a moderate heat.
Add the finely chopped onions.
Cook until the onions are soft. Do not colour.
Add to the finely crushed ingredients.
Cook for three minutes on a slow heat.
Season to taste.

Cucumber Chutney

Ingredients

1 cucumber
2 chillies
  vinegar and oil
  seasoning

Method

Clean the cucumber leaving no pips.
Grate the cucumber.
Chop the chillies finely.
Add the vinegar, oil and seasoning.
Mix all the ingredients together.

Coconut Chutney

Ingredients

1   grated coconut
3   red chillies
10 mint leaves
4   coriander leaves
    seasoning

Method

Roast the coconut until a light brown.
Ensure all ingredients are dry.
Place all ingredients together in a liquidizer.
Grind together until a paste is formed.

Chinese Cooking

a totally fulfilling experience

The Chinese in Mauritius have always been in a minority. However, they have not only preserved their rich culinary heritage but have succeeded in sharing it with fellow members of the Mauritian community. It is perhaps the inherent adaptability of Chinese cuisine itself which accounts for the fact that it has been readily accepted and appreciated wherever the Chinese immigrants took it — be it to London or San Francisco, Sydney or Samarkand.

The islands of the Indian Ocean are no exception. Chinese cuisine in Mauritius has been modified to take local ingredients into account. Thus, alongside familiar Chinese favourites like soya sauce, root ginger, bamboo shoots, cornflour and dried mushrooms, you will observe the occasional infiltration from another culinary world of tamarind and chilli powder, coconut and cream, pineapple and peanuts. It is these local touches that make some of our Chinese recipes unusual and unique. The spirit of trial and adventure which shapes all Chinese cooking makes the inclusion of unconventional elements perfectly legitimate.

Though ingredients can vary according to local taste and availability, the general principles and techniques which inform Chinese cuisine are universally respected. All Chinese dishes require lengthy preparation beforehand, but quick cooking. Vegetable oil and oil made from roasted sesame seeds are often used because they reach high temperatures quickly, whereas butter is almost always excluded. A coating of hot oil over meat and vegetables serves, in fact, to seal in taste and nutritive value.

Stir frying, used in the making of spring rolls (page 81) and Cantonese rice (page 92), is a common technique in Chinese cooking. Here crispness is the main criterion. The ultimate failure is food which is soggy and overcooked. The maximum time for stir frying is three to five minutes. Food which has been quickly stir fried must be eaten with the same haste.

The deep frying technique used in the making of stuffed crab claws (page 85), and which involves coating with cornflour, is also part of standard procedure. Whenever food is deep fried it is imperative to drain well and serve at once.

Chinese food is often steamed (buns and pancakes, pages 80 and 90) by placing the ingredients on a plate and the plate on a small rack. The plate and rack are then put into a pot containing a little water. The pot is covered and the water boiled. The steam from the water cooks the food on the plate. The water level must be well below that of the plate to avoid water spilling into the ingredients.

The Chinese in Mauritius, like their brothers scattered all over the globe, use a small range of simple tools and utensils — a wok (a round-bottomed heavy metal pot with two small handles), ladles and fish slices, drainers and steamers, and a heavy chopper or cleaver with an accompanying wooden chopping board. The cooked food is eaten of course with chopsticks out of small bowls and washed down with China tea — a necessary digestive.

The size of the bowls allows for 'sampling' and relishing of all the nine to fourteen courses that follow in carefully planned succession. The sequence of dishes is dictated by the need for contrast — cold followed by hot, solid by liquid, crisp after tender, thick after watery, subtle after sharp and so on. The Chinese, however, have very few desserts. In Mauritius a black jelly (*mousse noire*) or a fruit salad is served.

Lychees are often an important part of such a salad, or eaten fresh on their own. They are a fruit that grows well in Mauritius in the summer months between November and February. Each fruit, slightly bigger than a ping-pong ball, has a rough strawberry-red shell and juicy white flesh enclosing a smooth brown seed. The shell is brittle which makes it easy to peel. The lychee tree can reach a height of forty feet and is truly magnificent when laden with its heavy red fruit. Because of their seasonal nature, tinned lychees are sometimes served in restaurants. These are almost as tasty as the fresh variety. The intricacy and delicacy which characterise Chinese script, scroll painting, cloisonné and ivory carving extend to the preparation and presentation of food. Vegetables and fruit are chiselled into floral shapes and symmetrical patterns, meat is sliced paper thin, pastry is rolled until it is transparent, fish balls are gently moulded in the palm of the hand and fruit salads served in the decorated shells of watermelons. The final effect of Chinese food, laid out course after fascinating course on a hand-embroidered tablecloth, is one that appeals to all the senses. The act of eating thus becomes a totally fulfilling experience.

Coconut Milk

Thick coconut milk

Coconut milk can be bought as compressed cakes.
These are dissolved in warm water to the required
thickness. If they are not available, there are three
different ways of obtaining the same results suggested
below.

1. Take 150 g fresh coconut and break into small
   pieces removing the brown skin.
   Place in a liquidizer with one or two cups of water
   or milk.
   Grind on a high speed until a smooth liquid is
   obtained.
   Strain through muslin. The result is thick coconut
   milk.
2. For thin coconut milk add a further two cups of
   hot milk or water before putting through
   muslin.
3. Fresh coconut milk can be frozen into cubes.
   Use as many cubes as is necessary.

Cha Shao Pao

Steamed pork buns

Ingredients for paste

150 g sifted plain flour
2   lightly beaten eggs
¼   litre cold water

Ingredients for filling

2   cabbages
½   kg finely minced pork
2   tots Chinese rice wine or
     dry sherry
2½   teaspoons soya sauce
2   g salt
3   g sugar
5   g cornflour
3   tablespoons finely
     chopped bamboo shoots

Method

Place the flour and salt in a bowl.
Make a well and pour the eggs and water into it.
Mix into a smooth paste.
Knead the dough for five minutes.
The dough must be smooth and soft.

Method

Wash and clean the cabbages, removing the stalks.
Cut the cabbages into very fine dice.
Mix with the bamboo shoots.
Place the rest of the ingredients in a bowl and
mix thoroughly.
Stir in the cabbage and bamboo shoots.
To fill each bun, roll and cut the pastry into 6½ cm
rounds.
Place the pastry into the palm of your hand.
Form a cup with your hand and place a tablespoon of
mixture into the centre of the pastry.
Gather the sides of the pastry around the filling
towards the centre.
Squeeze the middle gently to make sure the pastry fits
around the filling.
Tap the base of the bun to flatten, so that it stands
upright.
Place on a greased tray and cover with plastic
wrapping.
Refrigerate for thirty minutes.
Place in a steamer and steam for thirty minutes over a
high heat.
Serve hot.
Many varieties of filling may be used.

Spring Rolls

Ingredients

3	eggs
220	g flour
5	g salt

Method

Break the eggs into a bowl with a little salt and
and beat lightly.
Sieve the flour and salt together.
Add the eggs to the salt and flour and form a smooth
pastry.
Place on a floured board and knead gently for five
minutes.
The pastry will become elastic and easier to roll.
When kneading is completed, cover with a damp
cloth.
Let the pastry rest for a good ten minutes.
Take a piece of dough and place on a floured board.
With a floured rolling pin press down on the pastry as
firmly as possible and roll hard.
This makes the pastry thin and transparent.
This is absolutely essential.
Take care not to break the pastry.
Cut it into squares 15 cm across and cover with a
damp cloth.
Proceed with the remaining dough as above.
When completed cut the squares into two triangular
shaped pieces.

Spring Roll Filling

Ingredients

6   chopped water chestnuts
4   minced spring onions
8   soaked Chinese
    mushrooms
100 g lightly fried minced
    pork
1   grated carrot
50 g beanshoots
50 g chopped raw
    prawns
20 g cornflour
5   g salt
1½ tablespoons dark soya sauce
10 g white sugar
2   cloves crushed garlic
8   fresh coriander leaves
    oil for frying

Method

Chop the coriander leaves finely.
Soak the Chinese mushrooms in water for twenty minutes, then cut them into shreds.
Blanch the beanshoots in boiling water for one minute.
Drain and cool.
Place all the ingredients together in a bowl, with the exception of the oil, and mix well.
Place the oil in a pan and heat on a fast heat.
Put all the ingredients into the pan and cook for two minutes.
Stir fry to prevent burning.
Allow to cool.

Filling the spring roll

Place a heaped tablespoon of filling on each triangular piece of pastry.
Turn in the two ends and fold the pastry over, to form a roll.
Stick the third end down with water.
When completed, refrigerate for half an hour, to allow the rolls to rest.
Heat the oil for deep frying and dip spring rolls into the oil.
Fry until golden brown and drain.
Before serving return to the hot oil for half a minute to crispen.
Serve with soya sauce.

Sweet Peanut Soup

Ingredients

200 g roasted peanuts
16   g sesame seeds
        (known locally as
        gingeli)
10   cups water
125 g white sugar
50   g cornflour
½   cup thick cream

Method

Toast the sesame seeds.
Grind the seeds and peanuts together to a fine
powder.
Add a little of the water if required.
Place all the ingredients in a pan with the exception of
the cream and the cornflour.
Stir well and simmer until of a very smooth
consistency.
Strain well.
Replace in a pan and bring to the boil.
Mix the cornflour with the cream and make a smooth
paste.
Stir into the soup and continue to stir until the soup
thickens.
Serve warm.

Fishball Soup

Ingredients for the fish balls

400 g of barracuda (known
     locally as *Tazar*)
5   g fresh coriander leaves
5   chopped spring onions
3   g salt
1   g white pepper
2   tablespoons oil

Method for the fish balls

Remove any bones and skin from the fish.
Chop the flesh finely.
Chop the coriander leaves very finely.
Mix the coriander, onions, salt and pepper together
with the fish.
Mix to a very smooth paste with the oil and knead
well. Add a little cold water.
Oil your hands and form the paste into small balls.
Do this by squeezing the paste in a clenched hand,
between the thumb and curled forefinger.
When complete, drop the fish balls into a bowl of cold
salted water.

Ingredients for the soup

¼   litre fish stock
2   g chilli powder
3   g grated root ginger
300 g cabbage or mustard
     greens finely shredded
1   finely chopped chilli
    oil

Method for the soup

Place a little oil in a pan to heat.
Place the ginger, cabbage and chilli in the oil.
Stir fry for one minute over a fast heat.
Boil the fish stock and chilli powder for one minute.
Add the fried items to the stock and boil for one
minute.
Gently drop the fish balls into the soup and cook for
five minutes.
When the fish is cooked, serve piping hot.
Sprinkle some chopped coriander leaves on top prior
to serving.

Stuffed Crab Claws

Ingredients

6   crab claws
200 g raw peeled prawns
1   egg white
1   egg
5   g dry English mustard
50   g fresh white bread crumbs
     juice of 1 lemon
     toasted sesame seeds
     cornflour
     oil for deep frying
     seasoning

Method

Clean the prawns and grind or mince them to a fine paste.
Add the breadcrumbs and mix in well.
Add the egg white, lemon juice and mustard.
Again mix in well.
Season to taste.
Break the shell from the crab claws very carefully.
Leave the meat attached to the central sinew inside the crab meat.
Press the ground prawns mixture around the crab meat.
Leave the tip of the claw exposed.
Beat the egg with a little salt.
Coat the meat very lightly with cornflour.
Brush with the egg and dip into sesame seeds.
Coat again with cornflour.
Place the oil on to heat.
Deep fry the claws for about three minutes.
Drain well and serve immediately.

Fried Chilli Prawns

Ingredients

500	g large prawns
1	sliced onion
2	cloves crushed garlic
5	g grated root ginger
1	grated lemon rind
1	cup thick coconut milk (page 79)
5	chopped spring onions
2	sliced tomatoes
5	g chilli powder
2	sliced green chillies
10	g tamarind
½	cup water
	peanut oil for frying

Method

Soak the tamarind in the water.
Peel and clean the prawns leaving the heads and tail intact.
Heat the oil in a pan.
Fry the onions and garlic together until soft. Do not colour.
Add the prawns and cook for two minutes.
Add the ginger, lemon rind, tomatoes, chillies and chilli powder and cook for two more minutes.
Pour on the coconut milk and simmer for two minutes.
Strain the tamarind water into the above.
Add the chopped spring onions and season to taste.
Heat and serve immediately.

Ginger Prawns

Ingredients

500	g large prawns
1	teaspoon sesame oil
1	fresh pineapple
10	g grated ginger root
5	g ground black pepper
2	tablespoons white wine
	seasoning
	oil for deep frying

Method

Clean and peel the prawns.
Wash well and dry.
Season and roll in the finely grated ginger.
Allow to stand for ten minutes.
Place oil for deep frying in a pan and heat.
Deep fry the prawns until cooked.
When cooked, remove from oil and drain well.
Take care not to overcook the prawns otherwise they will become tough and dry.
Clean and chop the pineapple into chunks.
Place remaining ingredients into a pan and heat.
Return the prawns to the above ingredients and heat together.
Serve on a dish with prawn crackers.

Sweet and Sour Dorado

Ingredients

400 g dorado
5   g salt
    cornflour
1   large onion
50 g bamboo shoots
1   green pepper
½   cup light chicken stock
1   fresh crushed chilli
10 g grated root ginger
3   young corn shoots
4   cloves crushed garlic
5   fresh mint leaves
50 g carrots
    oil for frying

For the sauce

½   cup vinegar
80 g brown sugar
2   tablespoons soya sauce
10 g cornflour
1   tablespoon honey

Method

Cut the fish fillets to the required size.
Season and cover lightly with a little cornflour.
In a saucepan combine all the ingredients for the sauce except for the cornflour.
Bring to the boil.
Mix the cornflour with a little cold water to form a paste.
Thicken the sauce with the cornflour.
Stir well on a high heat until the sauce clears.
Remove from the heat.
Cut the onion, carrots, bamboo shoots, young corn and pepper into julienne.
Place in a pan with water and boil for two minutes.
Add the ginger, garlic and chillies to the pan and cook for a further two minutes.
Add this to the sauce.
Place the oil in a pan and heat on moderate heat.
Fry the fish in the oil.
When cooked, remove from the pan and dry the oil from the fish.
Arrange on a dish and pour the hot sauce and vegetables over the fish.
Garnish with fresh mint leaves.
As an extra, tinned Chinese vegetables, 'sweet and hot', can be added.
Also as a garnish use fried mee foon sprinkled on top of the fish and sauce at the last moment.

Note:
This recipe can be used for any shellfish, pork, chicken or beef.

Chicken in Coconut Sauce

Ingredients

500 g boned chicken
3   g salt
1   g white pepper
1   finely chopped onion
1   cup chicken stock
4   crushed cardamoms
3   cloves crushed garlic
5   g ground coriander
     seeds
5   g grated root ginger
5   chopped spring onions
2   g chopped coriander
     leaves
40   g brown sugar
½   cup thick coconut milk
     (page 79)
½   cup oil
10   ground candlenuts
5   g dried shrimp paste

Method

Cut the chicken into bite size pieces.
Season with the salt and pepper.
Grind to a paste the chopped onion, ginger, garlic, cardamom, coriander, candlenuts and shrimp paste.
Heat the oil in a pan on a fast heat.
Place the spiced paste in the oil and cook for three minutes.
Add the chicken and cook until well coloured.
Pour in the chicken stock, stir well and bring to the boil.
Simmer for a further three minutes, adding more stock if required.
Pour in the coconut milk and brown sugar.
Cook until sauce thickens.
Garnish with the chopped spring onion.
Serve with freshly stir fried mange tout.

Vegetable Omelette

Ingredients

60 g bamboo shoots
20 g soaked
      Chinese mushrooms
1   grated carrot
10 g grated root ginger
8   spring onion shoots
5   eggs
15 g cornflour
2   tablespoons water
1   teaspoon sesame oil
1   sprig fresh coriander
      leaves
1   fresh red chilli (optional)
60 g roast pork
15 g bean shoots
½   teaspoon soya sauce
      oil for frying
      seasoning

Method

Cut the bamboo shoots and roast pork into fine shreds.

Chop the spring onions into small pieces.

Beat the eggs lightly with a little salt, and season.

Add the sesame oil to the eggs.

Mix the cornflour with the water and add to the egg mix.

Place the oil in a pan on a fast heat.

Place the vegetables and pork in the pan with the soya sauce.

Fry lightly until the vegetables are slightly softened.

Pour in the eggs and stir the vegetables evenly through the egg.

Cook on low heat until omelette is firm underneath.

Turn omelette over and cook on the other side.

When cooked garnish with sprig of fresh coriander leaves and a chopped red chilli.

Rolled Egg and Pork Pancake

Tan Chuan

Ingredients for the filling

250 g finely minced pork
1½   teaspoons soya sauce
2½   teaspoons dry sherry or
        Chinese rice wine
1   lightly beaten egg
     salt

Ingredients for the pancake

4 eggs
  groundnut oil

Method

Combine pork, soya, beaten egg, salt and sherry.
Mix thoroughly together.
Mix the remaining eggs together with a fork.
Heat frying pan on moderate heat.
Coat bottom of pan with oil.
Pour half the beaten eggs into the pan.
Form a pancake with the egg in the pan.
Pour any residue of uncooked egg from the pan.
As soon as the pancake is firm, transfer it to a plate.
Repeat the process, making another pancake.
Place a spoonful of the pork and soya mix along the length of the pancake.
Roll the pancake tightly as for a Swiss roll.
Seal the edges with egg and press firmly together.
Steam the pancakes for twenty minutes.
Remove from the steamer. Cut into slices diagonally.
Serve hot or cold.

Chinese Noodles

Ingredients

500 g Chinese noodles
   (mine)
100 g chopped Chinese
   garlic (queue l'ail)
100 g grated carrot
100 g finely shredded
   cabbage
2   lightly beaten eggs
10 g crushed peppercorns
1   tablespoon dark soya
   sauce
4   soaked and sliced
   Chinese mushrooms
   oil for frying
   seasoning

Method

Lay Chinese noodles on to the table.
Separate with the fingers to ensure that the mine do not stick together.
Place the oil in a pan to heat.
Pour in the egg and cook well on both sides.
Remove from the pan and cut into julienne.
Sprinkle the soya sauce and peppercorns over the mine.
Mix in well.
Add all the other ingredients to the mine and mix well.
Place mine into a pan on a moderate heat.
Cook for approximately five minutes.
Stir fry frequently to ensure all the ingredients are heated through.
Season to taste.
More soya may be added if required.
For that 'little extra' chopped pork, beef or prawns can be added to the mine.
Serve immediately from the pan. Sprinkle with a little of the Chinese garlic.

Cantonese Rice

Ingredients

800 g cooked white rice
2   .eggs
60   g peeled prawns
60   g roast pork
1   large onion
4   spring onions
20   g Chinese mushrooms
     soya sauce
1   teaspoon sesame oil
6   fresh coriander leaves
60   g cooked beef
30   g chopped Chinese
     garlic (queue l'ail)
30   g grated carrot
15   g shredded white
     cabbage
20   g sugar
     oil for frying

Method

Soak the Chinese mushrooms for twenty minutes.
Finely chop the onion.
Beat the eggs with a little salt.
Chop prawns, beef and pork into small dice.
Finely chop the spring onions.
Fry the rice in the oil until the grains are well coated.
Put to one side.
Place the eggs in an oiled pan.
Swirl around the pan to form a pancake.
Cook until firm. Remove from the pan and cut into strips.
Cook prawns until pink. Remove from the pan.
Place the beef and pork in an oiled pan. Heat for thirty seconds.
Add the vegetables and cook for one minute.
Add extra oil if required.
Slice the mushrooms finely and add to the vegetables.
Stir fry for one minute.
Splash in the soya sauce and add the sugar.
Add the rice and prawns to the rest of the ingredients.
Stir fry again on a moderate heat until hot.
Transfer to a serving dish.
Place the strips of egg and coriander on top of the rice.

French Cooking

an invaluable tradition

Mahé de Labourdonnais was said to be a gourmet, making sure that, despite the trials and tribulations of the Isle de France, it was well stocked with French favourites — truffles, goose and Gruyere cheese, Champagne, Graves and Moscatel. His ancestors still living on the island continue to maintain high eating standards. The French traditional *penchant* for seafoods is given full rein in an island where these are readily available. But the *Bastille de la cuisine francaise* has been assailed by island insurgents who have succeeded in sprinkling their tropical spices, even in hallowed places. The oyster served with chilli (page 96) is a case in point.

In Mauritius there are basically two types of oyster. There is the wild oyster which is found in the region around Mahébourg in the south of the island. This oyster is caught very young, so is small and tasty. The larger oyster, *cucculata forskali,* is cultivated in special reserves. It is a low-tide oyster which grows fat and juicy and develops a more delicate flavour than its country cousin. It is in the winter months from mid-May to August that oysters are ready for the table. Unlike Europe, the months without 'r' are those in which the local oyster is available.

It is understandable that the delicacy of the oyster, the palm heart and the avocado appeals to the French palate. The Mauritian avocado begins to appear in the new year. Since the hard flesh quickly softens, many Mauritians knock the fruit off the trees when they are still unripe and allow them to mature in a sack of rice or on a sunny window sill. Once the fruit has ripened it bruises easily, making it necessary to consume it immediately the skin turns purple. A loose kernel within the fruit ensures that its buttery insides are ready to melt in your mouth. If cyclonic winds, common in the summer months, destroy the flowers or tiny fruit, the Mauritian nation is deprived of one of its most popular delicacies for a whole year.

Javanese deer, imported by the Dutch, are hunted only in the months of June, July and August. The male develops impressive antlers which are keenly sought after as trophies to be proudly hung on the timbered walls of elegant French colonial mansions. The deer are kept in fenced-in reserves on the edge of forests. The hunters sit in *miradors* — small raised platforms used as observation and vantage points for shooting. Bands of yelling beaters drive the thundering beasts out of the thickets straight to the open ground where the *miradors* have been erected. Although shooting is carefully controlled, a morning's kill could amount to several hundred pounds of flesh. Nearly 3,000 deer are shot every year. The *partie de chasse* is an occasion for good wine and food. Venison is often curried or served with pepper sauce (page 106). The liver is sometimes singled out for special treatment as in the recipe on page 107. The head of the young deer is sometimes turned into a magnificent galantine.

In true Mauritian style, there has been a profitable exchange of cooking ideas and eating habits between the local French community, only numbering about 10,000 citizens, and the other ethnic groups. The former have embraced diverse cuisines so whole-heartedly that the finest curries and most authentic *rougailles* may be relished in French households. So much so that a nineteenth century visitor to Mauritius remarked: 'They chew nutmeg and chillies as if they were sweets, and their pale features will hardly pink in the inferno of these condiments.'

In return the French have added to Mauritian cuisine a solid and valuable tradition of white and red sauces, mousses and cream soups, cheese and wine ingredients, patés and aspic and splendid displays of crab, *langouste* and *camaron*. The crunchy *pain 'maison'*, so central to the daily Mauritian menu, is undoubtedly of French inspiration. After 150 years of British rule, fried eggs and bacon are as alien to the ordinary Mauritian's breakfast table as ketchup on the Frenchman's. But the bread and tea or coffee formula of *petit déjeuner* is firmly entrenched in the *moeurs mauriciennes.* So too is the habit of setting a fine table resplendent, where possible, with family silver and Baccarat crystal, of tipping one's soup plate towards onself, of using the same knife and fork for several courses (remembering to rest them delicately on a special stand) and of serving cheeses before dessert. Mauritius does not officially celebrate French National Day. But in a sense it does.

Brochettes of Oysters

Ingredients

24 oysters
24 mushrooms
100 g white breadcrumbs
     juice of 1 lemon
1 pinch cayenne pepper
     Creole sauce (page 29)

Method

Poach, drain and remove the beards from the oysters.
Skewer them on small metal skewers with mushrooms
in between.
Pour over melted butter with lemon and seasoning.
Roll in fine white breadcrumbs with cayenne pepper.
Grill under a low heat.
Serve on rice with Creole sauce.

Spiced Oysters

Ingredients

24 oysters
1 teaspoon soya sauce
15 g sugar
40 g salted fish
10 g crushed root ginger
10 g crushed garlic
5 chopped spring onions
1 teaspoon dried
     shrimp paste
10 finely chopped
     fresh coriander leaves
½ teaspoon chilli powder
     juice of 2 lemons
½ cup of water
     oil for frying
     seasoning

Method

Clean the oysters by removing the beards. Keep the
shells apart.
Place salted fish in the liquidizer and make into a
purée with a little water.
Place the oil in a pan and heat.
Fry the onions, garlic and root ginger in the oil for
one minute.
Mix together the shrimp paste and dried fish purée.
Add the sugar, soya and chilli powder to the onions.
Fry for one minute.
Stir in the chopped coriander leaves.
Add water and simmer for a further minute.
Place the oysters in the pan and cook for three
minutes.
Add the lemon juice.
Replace the oysters in their shells.
Thicken the sauce with just a little cornflour.
Pour the sauce over the oysters which are now in
their shells.
Serve hot with lemon wedges.

Oysters with Chilli

Ingredients

24 oysters
2   spring onions
1   fresh chopped chilli
1   grated lemon rind
1   teaspoon dried lemon
        grass
4   lemon leaves, (lime may
        be used)
1   fresh chilli
    seasoning

Method

Place the oysters in about three cups of water and add the lemon grass, lemon rind, lemon leaves and seasoning.
Bring to boil until the oysters open. Put the shells on one side.
Remove oysters from the stock and clean them, removing the beards.
Place each oyster back into its base shell.
Strain the stock and reduce to half by bringing it to the boil.
Chop the spring onions, and clean and chop the chilli finely.
Add these to the stock which has now been reduced to half.
Boil for one minute.
Pour over the oysters and serve immediately.

Oysters Béarnaise

Ingredients

oysters
sauce béarnaise
prawns

Method

Open and clean the oysters, removing the beards.
Place on a tray and season.
Clean the prawns and cook in a court bouillon.
Allow two prawns per oyster.
When the prawns are cooked remove from the court bouillon.
Chop the prawns into two and place on to the oysters.
Cover with sauce bearnaise.
Place under grill to brown the béarnaise.
Serve immediately with lemon.

Oyster Fritters

Ingredients

24 oysters
60 g flour
1   egg
60 g white breadcrumbs
    Creole sauce (page 29)

Method

Break the egg into a bowl and whisk with a little salt.
Remove the oysters from the shells and clean,
removing the beards. Place them in the flour, then
into the egg and then roll the oysters into the white
breadcrumbs.
Place into hot fat and deep fry until golden brown.
Serve immediately with hot Creole sauce or sauce
tartare.

Oyster Soup

Ingredients

24   oysters
1   finely chopped onion
120 g butter
1   cup white wine
20   g flour
1   g cayenne
1   cup cream
     juice of 1 lemon

Method

Cook the finely chopped onions in 100 g butter until
soft but not brown.
Open the oysters and remove the beards.
Place the oysters in the pan with their liquor.
Add the white wine and lemon juice.
Bring to the boil.
Mix the flour, remaining butter and cayenne into a
paste.
Stir this paste into the liquor and whisk well. Boil
until the soup begins to thicken a little.
Pour the cup of cream into the soup and stir, taking
the soup off the boil.
Season to taste.

Palm Heart and Prawn Béarnaise

Ingredients

1   palm heart
    milk
40 peeled prawns
½   cup white wine
    sauce béarnaise
60 g butter
    seasoning

Method

Place the palm heart in sufficient milk to cover it.
Bring to the boil and simmer until the heart is soft
but still remains firm.
Take the heart out of the milk and dry.
Clean and cook the prawns in the white wine and
butter.
Season to taste.
Do not overcook the prawns as they become tough.
Slice the palm heart into 1 cm roundels.
Place the sliced palm heart on to a serving dish.
Place two prawns on top of each roundel of palm
heart.
If any liquor is left from the prawns, whisk it into the
béarnaise carefully.
Cover with sauce béarnaise and place under the grill
to brown a little.
Serve immediately.

Chicken Pâté in Aspic

Ingredients

1   kg chicken livers
2   large peeled and diced
    onions
2   cloves crushed garlic
1   teaspoon mustard
¼   teaspoon ground cloves
¼   teaspoon nutmeg
1   slightly beaten egg
1   tot port
1   tot brandy
1   boiled egg
4   eggs
20 g gelatine
¼   litre chicken stock
30 g melted butter
    oil for frying
    seasoning

Method

Warm the chicken stock and sprinkle the gelatine on top.
Whisk well until the gelatine is dissolved. Stand to one side.
Trim and wash the chicken livers well.
Place the oil in a pan and heat.
Add the chopped onions and garlic and cook for one minute.
Stir in the chicken livers and cook for a further five minutes.
Add the nutmeg, cloves and mustard and stir in.
Take off the heat and cool slightly.
Place into a liquidizer or press through a sieve until puréed.
Fold in the melted butter, brandy, port and beaten egg.
Chop the white of the boiled egg into a fine dice.
Fold this into the pâté.
Pour into a mould and cook in a moderate oven for one hour.
Remove from the oven and press with a weight.
Allow to cool.
When cool pour in the gelatine stock.
Chill for four hours prior to serving.
Turn out of the mould and cut into slices.
Serve with hot, crisp toast.

Palm Heart Vinaigrette

Ingredients

1 palm heart
   juice of 2 lemons
   vinaigrette
1 hard boiled egg
3 chopped spring onion tops

Method

Clean and prepare the palm heart.
Chop into very fine slices.
Add the juice of the lemons to prevent the palm heart going brown.
Chop the white of the hard boiled egg.
Add to the palm heart with the finely chopped onions.
Finally add the vinaigrette, just enough to coat the palm heart.
Blend in the palm heart and mix well.
Place in a piece of the palm bark and serve with half a lemon.
Serve immediately.

Avocado Mousse

Ingredients

2 large mashed avocados
1 chopped spring onion
1 cup cream
½ cup mayonnaise
½ cup hot water
1 teaspoon gelatine powder
½ tablespoon ground
    nutmeg
  juice of 1 lemon
  seasoning

Method

Place the mashed avocados in a bowl.
Add the lemon juice, salt, pepper, nutmeg and spring onion.
Fold the mayonnaise into the above mixture.
Put the hot water into a cup and sprinkle the gelatine on top.
Stir until dissolved and let cool.
Whisk the cream until thick.
Fold the cool gelatine into the avocado mix.
Fold in the whipped cream.
Spoon the mousse into a mould and chill for four hours.
When ready, turn out on to a platter.
To facilitate turning out, place the mould in hot water for thirty seconds.

Avocado Soup

Ingredients

5 large avocados
1 litre chicken stock
1 cup thick cream
1 rind of finely
    grated lemon
  juice of 1 lemon
  seasoning

Method

Peel and remove stones from the avocados.
Mash the flesh of 4½ pears keeping ½ an avocado apart.
Chop the ½ avocado into very fine dice. Toss in the lemon juice.
Bring the chicken stock to the boil.
When just about to boil remove it from the heat.
Whisk the avocado purée into the stock.
Fold in the lemon rind and cream.
Season to taste.
Chill for four hours.
Prior to serving add the diced avocado.
Serve very cold.

Crabs in Bouillon

Ingredients

125 g butter
1   onion
125 g tomato
10 g crushed root ginger
1   sprig fresh thyme
2   cloves garlic
1   teaspoon saffron
½   red pimento
2   medium sized boiled
      crabs
2   tablespoons tomato purée
2   litres fish stock
1   bay leaf

Method

Remove the white meat from the crab.
Cut into fine dice.
Crush the remaining parts of the crab.
Chop the onion finely.
Cut the tomato into pieces.
Put a quarter of the butter into a pan and heat (not too hot otherwise the butter will brown).
Add the onion, thyme, ginger, garlic, tomato purée and crushed crab.
Add to this the fish stock.
Let simmer slowly for about two hours.
When cooked, pass through a very fine strainer producing a fine sauce.
Cut the red pimento into a fine dice.
Warm the rest of the butter in a pan.
Add the crab meat, pimento and saffron.
Let cook for one minute and add the crab soup.
Serve hot in a tureen.
Croutons can be served with this soup.
A spiral of fresh cream may also be added to the soup prior to serving — and, of course, a tot of brandy.

French Baked Crab

Ingredients

90 g butter
500 g fresh crab meat
70 g fresh white bread-
        crumbs
1   green pepper
4   cloves crushed garlic
10 g cayenne pepper
5   g ground mace
2   crushed green chillies
10 g chopped parsley
2   tots sherry
    juice of 2 fresh limes.
    seasoning

Method

Finely chop the green pepper into shreds.
Shred the crab meat and mix with 30 g of bread-
crumbs.
Melt 30 g of butter in a pan.
Add the garlic, shredded green pepper and chillies.
Cook for one minute on a moderate heat.
Do not brown.
Remove the pan from the heat.
Stir in the sherry, lime juice, mace, parsley and season
to taste.
Add the entire contents of the pan to the crab and
breadcrumbs mixture.
Toss them together thoroughly but gently.
Transfer the mixture to a buttered pie dish.
Sprinkle the top with the rest of the breadcrumbs.
Dot the top with the remaining butter.
Bake in a moderate oven for thirty minutes until
lightly browned.
Serve at once.

Camarons with Rice

Ingredients

750 g shelled camarons
60   g bacon
2   finely chopped onions
3   finely chopped chillies
4   cloves crushed garlic
800 g long grain rice
10   tomatoes
625 ml chicken stock
     freshly grated cheese
     oil for frying
     seasoning

Method

Clean the camarons taking the vein from the back.
Cut the prawns into 1 cm pieces.
Cut the bacon into 1 cm pieces.
Peel the tomatoes, cut them in half and remove the seeds.
Finely chop the remaining flesh. Tinned tomatoes can be used as a substitute if required.
Heat the oil in a pan.
Fry the bacon pieces until crisp and brown.
Remove from the pan, drain and keep warm.
Drop the onions, chillies and garlic into the remaining fat.
Cook for one minute. Stir frequently and do not brown.
Add the rice and stir for a further two minutes.
Take care not to burn. Adjust the heat accordingly.
Stir in the chopped tomatoes and the chicken stock.
Bring to the boil over a high heat.
Season to taste.
Cover the pan tightly and simmer on a very low heat for five minutes.
Stir in the camarons, replace the lid and simmer for a further five minutes.
Most of the liquid should by now have been absorbed by the rice.
Taste for seasoning.
Fluff the rice up with a fork and put on to a heated dish.
Sprinkle the bacon on top.
Serve the grated cheese separately in a small bowl.

Camarons in Red Sauce

Ingredients

- 12 very large camarons
- ½ kg very red tomatoes
- 1 large onion
- 1 sprig fresh thyme
- 10 g parsley
- 10 g crushed root ginger
- 10 g crushed garlic
- 2 dessertspoons tomato paste
  hard boiled egg
  seasoning
  oil for frying

Method

Cook the camarons in a little water for a few seconds until they become red.

Clean and chop the onions very finely.

Remove the shell from the tail of the camaron.

Place the shell on a roche carri and crush until the shells become a powder.

Place two cups of water in a pan to boil with the powdered camaron shell.

Reduce until equivalent to one cup of liquid.

Strain this mixture through a piece of muslin.

Put this sauce to one side.

Blanch the tomatoes in boiling water and remove the skins and seeds.

Chop very finely.

Place the oil in a pan and heat.

Fry the onions taking care not to colour them.

Add the garlic, ginger and tomato paste and stir in well.

Fry for half a minute.

Add the camaron sauce to the onion mix.

Blend in the chopped tomatoes and stir well.

Add the spices and cook on low heat for five minutes.

Place the shelled camarons into the sauce and cook for a further five minutes on a gentle heat.

Slice the hard boiled egg.

Serve with rice and the sliced egg.

Venison Steak in Pepper Sauce

Ingredients

4	venison steaks
1	cleaned, chopped carrot
1	cleaned, chopped onion
½	cup olive oil
50	g flour
750	ml strong beef stock
30	g tomato purée
2	bayleaves
10	g parsley
1	celery stick
125	ml vinegar
125	ml red wine
20	g crushed peppercorns
10	g green peppercorns
50	g butter
100	g venison bones

Method

Place the olive oil in a pan to heat.
Brown the onion and carrot in the oil.
Sprinkle over the flour and brown it.
When the flour is browned add the tomato purée and stock.
Stir well to avoid any lumps.
Add the celery, bayleaf, parsley and bones.
Cover with a lid and simmer for 1½ hours.
Remove the lid and skim off excess fat.
Mix the vinegar, crushed peppercorns, red wine and green peppercorns.
Place in a separate pan and reduce until half its original volume.
Strain the brown sauce.
Pour the reduced vinegar and red wine mix into the brown sauce.
Simmer for a further thirty minutes.
Season to taste.
Cook the venison steak in a little oil.
Remove from the pan on to a dish.
Pour over the sauce and serve hot.
Cream and red currant jelly can be added to this sauce.

Venison Liver

Ingredients

90 g butter
1   minced onion
2   venison livers
30 g flour
1   cup red wine
30 g mushrooms
    juice of 1 lemon
20 g green peppercorns
    seasoning

Method

The liver of the venison must be really fresh.
Slice the liver very thinly.
Put into the red wine and peppers for 3 hours to marinate.
Slice the mushrooms.
Melt the butter in a pan and fry the onion for one minute.
Place the liver in the pan and cook each side for about one minute.
Remove the liver and keep warm.
Sprinkle the pan with the flour and stir.
Add the red wine and pepper marinade and stir well to form a smooth sauce.
Add the sliced mushrooms and simmer until fairly thick.
Pour in the lemon juice and season to taste.
Place the liver in the sauce and heat briefly.
Red currant jelly may be added to the sauce if desired.
Serve hot.

Saint Géran Specialities

the hallmark of international cuisine

The Saint Géran Hotel takes its name from the ship that sank off Mauritius in 1774, the ship that inspired the writing of the French novel *Paul et Virginie*. The hotel is situated on the north-east coast of the island not far from the site of the famous shipwreck. It has been built on a peninsula of filao and palm forest that sticks out into the sea like an index finger. With sea on three sides, the Indian Ocean is on permanent exhibition wherever you look. The architecture is characterised by openness — there are massive arches like those of a mosque or a Gothic cathedral; there are windows unfettered by shutters or draperies; there are verandahs framed only in bright bougainvillaea. The rooms have enormous sliding doors which allow you to breathe in sea and sun without stirring from your bedside.

When you decide to venture out into the tropical landscape, be it only to print the virgin sands with your footsteps, you will find the site and setting perfection itself. After having recovered from the shock of seeing a beach so white and a sea so green, you might wander through the landscaped gardens which encompass the white Moorish structures. Here *tilapia* fish slide hither and yon in translucent pools, indigenous trees and flowering shrubs vie for attention, and miniature waterfalls feed a freshwater lake. By this time you should be ready to get down to the serious business of treating your pigments to some badly needed ultra-violet, or fighting the flab with a touch of tennis, diving, water polo, sailing, fishing, *petanque* and golf. By the time that the failing light prevents you from doing all these things, the lights of the discothèque are already flashing, and the bonfires on the beach have attracted groups of hip-rolling sega dancers. The chrome of the casino lights stay bright long after the bonfires have died down.

Drinking — a central activity when sun and sea tickle your throat — takes place in the middle of the swimming pool. The main bar is in fact an island surrounded by a curvacious basin of sun-flecked water. Submerged bar-stools allow swimmers and frolickers to quench their thirst without clambering up on to the island-bar. A 'Planter's Punch' or 'Emerald Cooler' takes on a special quality when drunk waist-high in warm water.

Eating — a central activity when sun and sea tickle your taste buds — takes place on an alfresco terrace, or on verdant lawns between the pool and the sea, or under thatched beach-shades in a secluded corner of the gardens. To call the team of chefs, managers, waiters and waitresses friendly would be an understatement, a gross misrepresentation. Bubbling with energy and eagerness to please and inform, suggest and accommodate, they wear the sunshine of the island on their smiling faces. Here is the *gentillesse* of the French, without the formality, the efficiency of the British, without the reserve and the charm of the East without the language barriers. The staff of the Saint Géran, at a ratio of one member for every guest, is what makes this excellent hotel *hors concours*.

As for the hotel's specialities, the recipes and pictures speak eloquently enough for themselves. The master chef has taken the very best that Mauritius offers and stamped it with the hallmark of international cuisine. He has devised combinations that allow, say, the *vacoas* or *sacréchien* fish to be fully appreciated without the distracting additions of the heavy-handed enthusiast. The flavour and textures of palm heart and avocado come to the foremost in his entrées; beef steak, lamb and turkey show supremacy as *pièces de résistance.* Probably the most dramatic and memorable culinary endeavour is the *Langouste à la Saint Géran.* The *langouste* or crayfish is sometimes known as the spiny lobster. It looks like a lobster except for the pincers that it does not possess. It certainly turns that delicious red-orange in the pot or over coals. When the firm white flesh of *langouste* comes into carefully proportioned contact with avocados, mushrooms, cheese, egg yolk, nutmeg, lemon, black olives, thick cream and Pernod, the result is cataclysmic. Even the confirmed pessimist begins to feel relatively at peace with the world.

Avocat Belle Mare

Ingredients

30 g grated
     cheddar cheese
1   avocado pear
80 g crab meat
4   roundels palm heart
     red sauce (page 105)
50 g butter
2   tots brandy
     seasoning

Method

Cook 4 pieces of palm heart as mentioned in 'palm heart and prawn béarnaise' (page 98).
Make red sauce as mentioned in 'camarons in red sauce' (page 105).
Take the white meat from the crab and flake it.
Melt the butter in a pan.
Add the crab meat to the butter and cook gently.
Season to taste.
Add enough red sauce just to bind the crab meat together.
Add the brandy to the above.
Place the cooked palm heart on to a serving dish.
Peel and cut the avocado pear in half.
Remove the stone.
Cut the two halves in half again lengthways.
Turn the avocado pieces so that each piece is back to back as illustrated.
Put these pieces on to the palm heart roundels.
Place the crab meat in the middle of the pieces of avocado.
Cover the crab meat only with a little more heated red sauce.
Sprinkle the red sauce with the grated cheese.
Brown the cheese under a very hot grill for one minute.
Serve immediately.

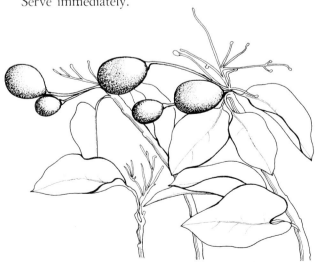

Crayfish Cocktail

Ingredients

1   crayfish
1   cup mayonnaise
1   orange
1   lemon
1   tot brandy
30 g tomato sauce
1   lettuce
1   coconut
    tabasco
    seasoning

Method

Cook the crayfish in boiling salted water for about twenty minutes. Allow to cool. Remove the meat from the tail of the crayfish. Chop into bite size pieces.

Cut the lemon in half and squeeze the juice of one half over the meat.

Mix the mayonnaise, brandy and tomato sauce together. Add a drop of tabasco.

Cut the orange in half and squeeze the juice into the sauce. Season to taste.

Chop the lettuce into fine shreds leaving two nice leaves whole.

Remove from the coconut as many coarse hairs as is possible.

Cut the coconut in half and place each half in a champagne glass.

Drop the shredded lettuce into the coconut shells. Place each whole lettuce leaf upright so as to show above the crayfish.

Mix the crayfish with half of the sauce.

Place the crayfish on top of the shredded lettuce.

Spoon sufficient sauce over the crayfish to cover it.

Decorate with a lemon slice, sliced hard boiled egg, picked parsley and two legs from the crayfish.

Paradise Cocktail

Ingredients

2   lettuces
     juice of 1 lemon
12   fresh water camarons
1   palm heart
     zest and juice of 2
        oranges
1   teaspoon tomato sauce
2   cups mayonnaise
2   boiled eggs
3   yellow coconuts
2   tots brandy
1   lemon
     tabasco
     seasoning

Method

Blend together the mayonnaise, tomato sauce, brandy and orange.
Boil the twelve camarons in a court bouillon.
Peel and clean six of these and cut into four.
Cut the coconuts in half, keeping the coconut water. (The coconut water is very pleasant when refrigerated and served with whisky or gin.)
Wash and dry the lettuce. Cut into very fine shreds.
Clean and cut the tails of the remaining six camarons up the centre and turn outwards so that the camaron stands upright. These will be used for decoration.
Take the softest part of the palm heart and chop finely. Add the brandy.
Pour the lemon juice on to the palm heart.
Cut the whites of the boiled eggs into julienne.
Fold the mayonnaise mixture into the palm heart. Work very quickly, otherwise the palm heart goes brown in colour. Add the chopped camarons.
Place the julienne of lettuce into the bottom of the coconut halves. On top add the palm heart mixture.
Decorate with tomato, slice of egg, lemon and decorative camarons.
Refrigerate for thirty minutes before serving.

Vacoas Ile Ronde

Ingredients for the fish

4 fillets of vacoas
2 cloves of chopped garlic
1 sprig thyme
1 bay leaf
1 glass white wine
1 glass fish stock
1 sliced onion
1 sliced carrot
1 celery stick
1 leek
  seasoning
  black peppercorns

Ingredients for the duxelle

20 g white breadcrumbs
150 g finely
      chopped mushrooms
150 g finely
      chopped onions
1   tot port
1   tot brandy
1   egg yolk
3   cloves garlic
60   g butter
     seasoning

Method for the fish

Place the fillets of fish on to a tray.
Add the rest of the ingredients to the fish.
Cover with oiled greaseproof paper and cook for approximately twenty minutes in a pre-heated oven.

Method for the duxelle

Crush the garlic.
Heat the butter in a pan.
Cook the onions and crushed garlic for one minute.
Do not brown.
Add the mushrooms and cook for two minutes.
Fold in the rest of the ingredients and stir fry for one minute. Remove from the heat.

Langouste à la Saint Géran

The LANGOUSTE is probably the most sought after and highly prized seafood in any country in the world.

The picture below depicts our famed LANGOUSTE À LA SAINT GÉRAN in the fine tropical setting of the Hotel from which it takes its name. The recipe can be found on the next page.

Ingredients

1	avocado pear
1	boiled langouste
½	finely chopped onion
100 g	sliced mushrooms
1	tot Pernod
1	sprig thyme
2	tablespoons spinach cooked in butter
150 g	butter
4	tablespoons thick cream
1	egg yolk
60 g	grated cheese
1	pinch nutmeg
1	lemon
	black olives
	seasoning

Method

Detach the tail from the head of the langouste.

Cut the langouste tail in half and remove the meat.

Peel the avocado pear, cut it in half and remove the stone.

With a parisienne cutter, cut the avocado pear into ball shapes.

Add the egg yolk to the cream and whisk to thicken a little.

Put the butter into a pan on a slow heat to melt.

Place the onions into the butter and cook for one minute. Do not colour.

Add the mushrooms and cook for a further one minute.

Cut the langouste tail into bite size pieces.

Blend the langouste pieces in with the mushrooms and onions.

Heat, stirring continually. Add the thyme.

Pour in the cream mix and fold into the langouste.

Take the pan off the heat. Season to taste. Add the nutmeg.

Stir in 20 g of grated cheese and the Pernod.

Remove the sprig of thyme.

Chop the cooked spinach and place into the bottom of the two tails.

Spoon the langouste on top of the spinach.

Sprinkle the remaining grated cheese over the top and brown under a hot grill.

Place the two tails on a platter and decorate with the avocado balls.

Serve hot decorated with lemon, langouste head and black olives.

Sacréchien Tropical Style

Ingredients

5   fillets of sacréchien
1   cleaned and diced
        small pineapple
15   fresh or tinned stoneless
        cherries
5   g grated ginger
30   g diced cucumber
1   diced banana
1   diced apple
     flour
100 g butter
5   halves of lemon
3   chopped mint leaves
     seasoning

Method

Take fillets and sprinkle with flour and seasoning.
Melt 30 g of butter in a pan on a moderate heat.
Fry the fish in the pan. Do not colour.
Take the fish out of the pan.
Melt the rest of the butter in the pan until hot.
Add the diced cucumber, fruit, ginger and mint leaves.
Place the hot fish on a platter.
Spoon the garnish and butter mix over the fish.
Serve with the halves of lemon.

Fresh Water Camarons

Ingredients

6   king size camarons
1   cup dry white wine.
1   chopped onion
60 g butter
1   lemon
1   clove crushed garlic
    seasoning

Method

Split the tails of the camarons and remove the black vein.
Wash and dry. Ensure the heads are kept intact.
Melt the butter in the pan and add the white wine, onion and garlic.
Place the camarons into the butter and wine and cook for five minutes.
Turn the camarons over to cook the other side.
Cook for a further five minutes.
Squeeze the juice of half a lemon on to the camarons.
When the camarons are cooked remove from the pan.
Season the residue left in the pan.
Serve the camarons on a bed of rice.
Pour the residue over the camarons.
Decorate with the remaining lemon, peeled parsley and radish.

Fillet of Sacréchien Trou d'Eau Douce

Ingredients

4	fillets of sacréchien
2	bananas
60	g blanched whole almonds
1	sprig fresh thyme
1	bay leaf
1	cup white wine
1	tablespoon vinegar
250	g butter
60	g chopped cucumber
	juice of 1 lemon
	seasoning

Method

Remove all bones and skin from the fish fillets.
Season with salt and pepper.
Place the wine, thyme, bay leaf, vinegar and
100 g butter in pan. Place the fish in this liquor.
Cover with greaseproof paper. Bring to the boil and
simmer gently for four minutes.
When the fish is cooked, take it off the heat and
remove from the liquor.
Peel and chop the bananas. Skin and chop the almonds.
Place the rest of the butter into a pan on a fast fire.
Cook the butter until a light nut-brown. Take off the
heat immediately and pour in the lemon juice.
Add the banana, almonds and cucumber to the butter.
Place the hot fish on to a platter and pour the sauce
over it. Serve with lemon stars and picked parsley.

Fillet Steak 'Isle de France'

Ingredients

3   fillets steaks, trimmed to
      desired size
1   finely chopped onion
1   tot drambuie
1   tablespoon horseradish
      sauce
1   cup beef stock
½   cup white wine
5   g basil
1   bay leaf
10 g tomato purée
10 g flour
¼   cup cream
10 g butter
      oil for frying

Method

Heat the oil in a pan.
Add the finely chopped onions. Cook for one minute
but do not colour.
Sprinkle the flour over the onions and stir in well.
Pour in the white wine and cook for two minutes
stirring well.
Stir in the tomato purée and the beef stock.
Stir well to prevent lumps from forming.
Add the bay leaf and basil. Cook until it has reduced
to ⅔ of its original volume and is a smooth sauce.
Add the horseradish. Stir into the sauce.
Cook for one minute.
Pour in the drambuie and stir in the butter at the last
moment.
Take off the heat and cover.
Cook the fillets in a separate pan to the desired
degree.
Serve the fillets with the sauce immediately.

Noisette d'Agneau Marie-France

Ingredients

1	loin of lamb trimmed and boned
6	peeled and seeded tomatoes
3	chicken livers
1	cup dry red wine
250	g fresh mushrooms
2	onions
1	clove crushed garlic
2	tots port
1	cup sauce béarnaise
15	g flour
2	cups beef stock
30	g butter
15	g tomato purée
5	g rosemary
1	bay leaf
	olive oil for frying
	seasoning

Method

Chop one onion and the mushrooms into very fine dice. Melt the butter in a pan.

Add the onion and garlic to the butter and cook for one minute. Do not colour.

Stir in the diced mushrooms and cook for a further minute.

Pour in the port. Season to taste and remove from heat. Allow to cool.

Take the loin of lamb off the bone and trim off excess fat.

Lay the loin flat on the table.

Spoon the mushroom mix along the centre lengthways.

Roll the loin up so that the mushrooms form a filling.

Tie with string to keep the rolled loin in shape.

Refrigerate for thirty minutes to make the meat firm. This makes cutting easier.

Cut the loin into 2.5 cm pieces, ensuring that the string will keep the shape of each slice.

Season and sprinkle each piece with rosemary.

Chop the chicken livers into fine dice.

Place the oil in a pan and heat.

Cook the lamb in the oil for five minutes. Turn and cook for further five minutes.

Remove from the pan and put to one side.

Finely chop the remaining onion. Drop it in the oil and cook for one minute. Do not colour.

Add the chicken livers and cook for half a minute.

Sprinkle the flour over the onions and liver. Stir in well.

Add the tomato purée, beef stock and bay leaf.

Stir well to form a smooth sauce.

Reduce by half to serve.

Remove the string from each piece of lamb.

Place the hot lamb into a hot serving dish.

On each piece of lamb place a half of a tomato, previously seeded.

Cover the whole thing with the sauce.

Spoon the béarnaise over the tomato and lamb.

Place under grill to brown lightly.

Serve immediately with vegetables of your choice.

Noisette d'Agneau Florence

Method

Proceed exactly the same as Noisette Marie-France only replace the béarnaise sauce with a strong minted hollandaise sauce.

Fillet d'Agneau
Labourdonnais

Ingredients

6   fillets of trimmed lamb
1   finely chopped onion
20   g paprika
1   large green pepper
1   large red pepper
60   g sliced mushrooms
125   ml thick cream
2   tots calvados
2   glasses dry white wine
      oil for frying

Method

Cut the green and red peppers in half and remove the seeds.
Cut into fine julienne.
Roll the lamb fillets into the paprika.
Heat the oil in a pan on a moderate heat.
Cook the onion in the oil for one minute.
Do not colour.
Add the mushrooms and sliced peppers.
Cook for a further minute, stir frying all the time.
Place the lamb fillets in the pan and cook on all sides.
Pour in the white wine and allow to simmer for three minutes.
Blend in the thick cream and stir well.
Cook for a further two minutes. Do not boil.
The sauce will then start to thicken.
Add the calvados.
Season to taste.
Serve with white rice.

Escalope de Dinde Alicia

Ingredients

4   slices of raw turkey
      breast
2   slices of gruyère cheese
100 g white breadcrumbs
1   egg lightly beaten
50 g flour
50 g butter
      juice of 1 lemon
      seasoning
      oil for frying

Method

Place egg, flour and breadcrumbs into separate containers.

Take the 4 slices of turkey and flatten them.

Place a slice of cheese and a slice of ham on to two pieces of turkey.

Wet the edges of the turkey with a little of the egg.

Place the remaining two slices on top to cover the cheese and ham.

Press down the edges of the turkey. Season the top and bottom.

Dip the turkey into the flour, then into the egg.

Drain off any surplus egg from the turkey then place it into the breadcrumbs.

Cover the turkey top and bottom with the breadcrumbs.

Heat the oil in the pan over a moderate heat.

Place the escalopes into the oil and cook each side for approximately five minutes at a time.

The escalopes should be of a light golden-brown colour.

Care should be taken not to brown too much.

Remove from the pan.

Take the butter and boil for one minute until a very light brown.

Add the lemon juice.

Place the escalopes on to a platter and pour the butter over them.

Sirloin Steak Malagasse

Ingredients

3   sirloin steaks
½   cleaned and chopped pine-
      apple
10 g green peppercorns
30 g thick cream
10 g crushed black
      peppercorns
1   teaspoon red currant jelly
5   g crushed basil
1   clove crushed garlic
1   bay leaf
1   finely chopped onion
1   cup red wine
15 g flour
2   cups beef stock
     oil for frying
     seasoning

Method

Heat the oil in the pan.
Add the chopped onions and cook for one
minute.
Do not colour.
Sprinkle the flour over the onions and cook for
one minute.
Stir in the crushed peppercorns, garlic, green
peppercorns, bay leaf and red wine.
Cook for a further minute, stirring to prevent
lumps.
Pour in the beef stock, red currant jelly and bay
leaf.
Stir again to ensure a smooth sauce.
Reduce by cooking to half the original volume.
Stir in the cream and chopped pineapple.
Season to taste.
Cook the sirloin steaks in a separate pan to the desired
degree.
Place the steaks when cooked on to a heated platter.
Pour the sauce over the steaks.
Serve immediately with vegetables of your choice.

Fillet of Sacréchien Guylaine

Ingredients

1   fillet of sacréchien
60 g butter
½   glass dry white wine
30 g flour
3   asparagus tips
     juice of one lemon
     sauce à la Creole
     (page 29)
     sauce béarnaise
     seasoning

Method

Brush the fish with flour and season it.
Heat the butter in a pan.
Place the fish in the butter to cook for two
minutes.
Turn the fish over to cook the other side for a
further two minutes.
Add the white wine and continue cooking the fish.
When finally cooked remove from pan on to a
plate.
Pour the lemon juice over the fish.
Place the heated asparagus tips spaced apart on top of
the fish.
Heat the Creole sauce in pan.
Spoon the hot Creole sauce in between the asparagus
tips.
Cover the whole fish with sauce béarnaise and place
under the grill to brown.
Serve with assorted vegetables.

Barbecue Displays

food as an art form

Food displays at the Saint Géran make Harrods Food Hall look like the corner shop — piles of multi-coloured fruit, wicker fish traps full of wide-eyed barracuda, *crevettes* climbing up mountains of lettuce leaves like over-grown red ants, obese oysters on ice, mirrors of poached fish, and baskets of edible tropical greenery everywhere. And amidst the abundance stand sculptures, not of marble, but of pastry margarine carved into life-size figures of classical gods and legendary lovers, prehistoric bird-life and exotic marine creatures. But it is probably the dodo sculptures, each a superb study in dumpy dim-wittedness, that add an especially 'Looking-Glass' quality to the whole effect.

Each creation is worked out in the mind of the chef as a stick-figure, and a framework constructed out of pieces of light metal welded together and firmly attached to a base. This base serves as a stretcher for transporting the sculpture once it is complete. Around the all-important frame the form is built up with silver foil, crushed, smoothed, flattened, twisted and tied to give the subject bulk and movement. This can take up to four hours to achieve.

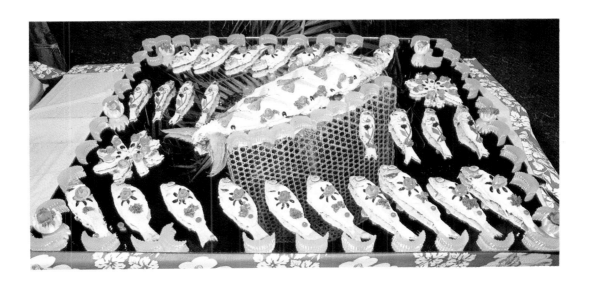

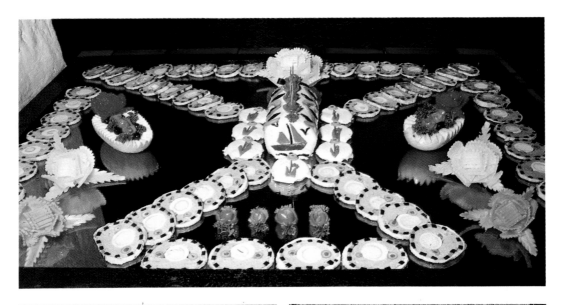

The larger sculptures involve anything up to 100 five-pound packets of pastry margarine. This softens at room temperature and is almost like plasticine by the time the chef is ready to start covering the foil with it. Using his bare hands he heaves, heaps, pushes and pummels until the ghostly silver paper undercarriage is completely covered in a rich cream paste. Surfaces are smoothed over by dipping the hands into hot water and stroking each bulge and

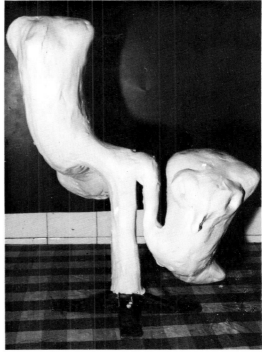

crevice until every little lump and surface imperfection sinks into the over-all shining rotundity. At some points the margarine is an inch thin, at others four inches deep. Details like scales, curls, claws, feathers and fingers are added with clay-carving tools. The actual modelling takes twelve hours, working for three-hour stretches.

Not only must the chef have an artist's eye for three-dimensional shapes and proportions, but also an instinct for timing and temperatures. If the sculpture stays refrigerated for too long it cracks; if it is overexposed to room temperature it becomes too soft to handle or simply develops affinities with modern sculpture — holes and all.

Many a dodo has relived its sad past by being treated to more than its fair share of tropical sunshine, or during a prolonged sojourn in a cooling compartment. When this happens, the item '500 lbs of pastry margarine' appears once again on the weekly shopping list.

With ice carving the problems are different, the results even less enduring. The chef must work inside a deep freeze where the temperature is 15 below at all times. The chosen motif, say a fish, is traced on to a block of ice of 3 feet long and hacked with a special saw. Components are sometimes carved from several standard blocks and fitted together with shavings of ice to form a single enormous structure. In the making of a huge ice bowl, for

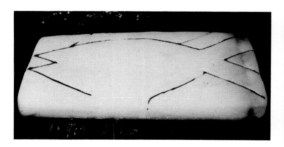

example, the main concave surface, the stem and the base, are all carved separately, and then mounted one on the other to form the general shape. The insides of the bowl are chiselled away till they are an inch thin in places. Hot irons are used to make indentations in the rim and decorative patterns on the surface. It takes forty-five minutes to make a bowl, three days to make a sailing ship. In both cases the chef can only work in the deep freeze for ten minutes at a stretch. If he goes beyond that limit the water freezes beneath his nails.

In constructing the Saint Géran ship, four blocks of ice are used to carve the hull; long ice bars are cornered off to make masts; trays of ice, one inch deep, are cut into the shapes of

billowing sails; and delicate bands of ice make up the rigging. It takes six men to carry in the crystal clipper, two to cart off the dripping shipwreck. Total life span: forty-five minutes.

It is during the open-air barbecues that the various carvings come into their own. Scattered over an area as wide as a football pitch the sculptures, a dozen in ice, a dozen in margarine, are given the kind of perspective needed to view them in their collective splendour. There are of course other decorations: waterfalls made of volcanic rock and decked with wild flowers; fountains spraying coloured vapour in all directions; *pirogues* loaded with fruit; chandeliers woven in palm leaves; and palm trees themselves brought in from a nearby plantation. In the centre are the barbecues — oil drums sawn in half, filled with charcoal and covered with metal grids. They are smokeless, but flare tempestuously when dripping or dressing hits the embers. The tables are covered in bright cotton materials, usually used for *pareos* or beach-wraps.

On the tables is a classic repertoire of marinated meats — *brochettes*, lamb cutlets, spicy sausages, honeyed chicken, minute steaks and suckling pig. There is also a selection of casseroles and curries. Seafoods range from the spectacular sight of 350 crayfish turning deep crimson over an open flame, to modest oysters quietly sizzling in white wine.

Barbecued fish abounds. One speciality is white tuna baked in foil and then allowed to simmer gently over the coals. *Dorades,* some of them weighing in at ten kilos, are grilled whole. *Rouget* or red mullet are small, but equally tasty when thoroughly charred on a red-hot grid. The firm flesh of marlin and shark lends itself to barbecuing, though care must be taken not to toughen it through overcooking.

Barbecued fish and meats are served with rice, piquant sauces and salads. A battery of salads

have been developed working on the principle that established combinations, like celery and pineapple, or green mango and chillies, or cucumber and mint, should form the basis of the salad, with elements like palm heart, pistachio nuts, caraway seeds, fresh herbs and brandy adding an original dimension to a well-known formula. Salads are thus built up, almost like 'lego', to produce something startlingly creative out of ingredients which are at once familiar and fanciful.

Guinea Fowl Egg Brochettes

Ingredients for the chicken meatballs

260 g chicken meat
2   egg whites
10   g sugar
3   teaspoons soya sauce
1   tot sweet sherry
     juice of 1 orange
     seasoning
     oil for frying

Ingredients for the brochettes

1   cucumber
12   guinea fowl eggs
12   small tomatoes
2   tablespoons vinegar
     salt

Method

Cook and finely mince the chicken meat and season to taste.

Blend the meat and egg whites to form a paste.

Form the meat into 24 meat balls.

Heat about 2.5 cm deep of oil in the pan.

Fry the meat balls in the oil until a golden brown.

Remove from the oil and drain.

Place the sugar, soya, sherry and orange juice in a pan.

Stir on a low heat until the sugar dissolves.

Return the meat balls to this sauce and turn them over in the sauce.

Simmer gently until the sauce forms a glaze over the meatballs.

Remove from the heat and allow the meat balls to cool.

Peel and remove the seeds from the cucumber.

Cut into 3.75 cm square cubes.

Marinate in vinegar and salt for ten minutes.

Boil the eggs for six minutes until hard.

Place under cold running water to cool straight away.

This stops the outside of the yolk from going black.

When the eggs are cold remove the shell.

Thread on to each skewer one meat ball, a piece of cucumber, one egg, one tomato and another meatball.

Heat on barbecue for two minutes.

Serve hot or cold with rice.

More sauce for the meatballs may be made and served over the brochettes, if required.

Lamb Cutlets

Ingredients

12   lamb cutlets
75   g freshly chopped mint
1   teaspoon rosemary
125   g brown sugar
1   litre vinegar
      seasoning
      water

Method

Trim the lamb cutlets, leaving very little fat.
Mix the rest of the ingredients together.
Let the cutlets marinate in this mixture for three hours.
Season and grill them on the barbecue.
Boil and reduce the marinade by one half. Strain it and serve separately.

Prawn Brochettes

Ingredients

48   prawns
1   cucumber
1   pineapple
100   g butter
2   cloves crushed garlic
10   g crushed root ginger
1   sprig thyme
1   bay leaf
1   tot brandy
      seasoning

Method

Melt the butter and add the brandy.
Add the garlic, ginger, thyme and bay leaf and mix well.
Peel and clean the prawns.
Allow 8 prawns per person using two brochettes.
Place the prawns into the butter mix and leave for two hours in the refrigerator.
Peel the skin off the cucumber.
Cut in half and remove all the seeds.
Cut the cucumber into pieces the same size as the prawns.
Peel and cut the pineapple in the same way.
Remove the prawns from the marinade.
Place the prawns on to the brochette with a piece of cucumber and pineapple between each prawn.
Season to taste.
Place the prawns on to a low heat barbecue.
Serve the brochettes on a bed of rice.
Heat the remaining brandy butter and serve separately.

Prawn and Sugarcane Brochettes

Ingredients

6	pieces fresh sugar cane 27 cm long
800 g	peeled prawns
30 g	fish sauce
2	egg whites
8	finely chopped spring onions
	oil
	seasoning

Method

Trim the cane 10 cm from each end to make the ends thinner than the centre.

Chop the prawns finely, season and add the fish sauce.

Season to taste.

Bind the prawns with the egg white.

Make into a smooth paste.

Press about 1 cm thick of the paste on to the centre of the cane.

Brush with the oil.

Place on the barbecue and cook for five minutes.

Turn continuously.

Remove from the barbecue and brush with oil again.

Dip the prawn mix into the chopped spring onions, coating the prawn mix lightly.

Press the onions on to the mix.

Return to the barbecue for another minute.

Ingredients for the sauce

60 g	brown sugar
20 g	sugar cane juice
20 g	fish sauce
30 g	crushed roasted peanuts
3	cloves crushed garlic
1	fresh red chilli minced

Method for the sauce

Mix the sugar, cane juice and fish sauce together.

Place in a pan on a low heat.

Stir until the sugar dissolves.

Blend in the peanuts, garlic and chilli.

Stir in a little water.

Cook for one minute.

Serve with the brochettes.

Beef Brochettes

Ingredients

450 g sirloin of beef
24 very small tomatoes
24 mushrooms
24 cleaned shallot onions
10 g butter
10 g flour
   seasoning

Ingredients for the marinade

1 bottle red wine
1 sprig fresh thyme
1 teaspoon marjoram
1 bottle barbecue sauce
2 bay leaves
¼ litre oil
1 teaspoon green peppercorns

Method

Mix together ingredients for the marinade.
Trim all the fat off the beef.
Cut the beef into 2 cm cubes.
Place the cubes of beef into the marinade and leave for four hours in the refrigerator.
Allow eight pieces of beef per person, using four on each brochette.
Remove the beef from the marinade.
Place the beef on to the brochettes with the tomatoes, mushrooms and shallots in between each piece.
Cook the brochettes on a low heat.
Season to taste.
For the sauce, strain the marinade.
Make a paste with the butter and flour.
Bring the wine to the boil and thicken with the butter paste.
The sauce should be just thick enough to coat one's finger.
Serve the brochettes on a bed of rice and cover with the sauce.

Minced Beef Brochettes

Ingredients

200 g minced beef
4   spring onions
1   cleaned carrot
1   cleaned green chilli
5   g basil
5   g marjoram
1   clove garlic
5   g root ginger
1   egg
    Lee and Perrins sauce
    seasoning

Method

Place all the items together and mince very finely.
Roll into a thin sausage and skewer with the
brochettes.
Cook on the barbecue and serve with barbecue sauce.
Mutton may also be used instead of the beef.
When using mutton add a little rosemary to the mix.

Chicken on a Spit

Ingredients

2   chickens
1   jar honey
1   cup vinegar
1   teaspoon oregano leaves
1   teaspoon rosemary
2   bay leaves
½   spoon butter
    seasoning

Method

Melt the honey and the butter together.
Add the rest of the ingredients.
Remove the intestines and wash out the chicken.
Season the chicken inside and out.
Tie the chicken with string; the wings should be tied
under the backbone and the legs tied together.
Marinate in the honey mixture for one hour in the
refrigerator.
Remove the chicken from the honey mixture and
place on the barbecue.
Rotate over the heat of the barbecue.
Continue brushing with the honey mixture every five
minutes.
Cooking time for a 1.5 kg chicken is approximately
thirty minutes on the spit.

Spare Ribs

Ingredients

1½	kg pork spare ribs
60	g brown sugar
3	cloves garlic
3	tablespoons dark soya sauce
3	tablespoons honey
30	g tomato paste
2	tablespoons sherry
½	teaspoon allspice
½	teaspoon nutmeg
1	teaspoon vinegar

Method

Trim the spare ribs neatly at ends.
Mix the remaining ingredients together.
Place the spare ribs into the mixed marinade.
Ensure the ribs are covered with the mixture.
Allow to marinate for four hours.
Place ribs on barbecue on a low heat.
Cook through until crispy on the surface.
Brush with the marinade liquid whilst cooking.

Peanut Salad

Ingredients

120	g cheddar cheese
1	pineapple
4	celery stalks
30	g roasted peanuts
1	cup fresh cream
	juice of 1 lemon
	seasoning
	sugar

Method

Clean the celery and cut into dice.
Cut the cheese and pineapple into dice.
Mix the above together and add the peanuts and sugar.
Pour the cream on to the salad and fold in.
Blend in the lemon juice. This has the effect of thickening the cream.
Season to taste.
Fruit yoghurt may be used in the place of the cream.

Tomato Salad

Ingredients

10 tomatoes
1   onion
2   green peppers
1   lemon
50 g sugar
5   spring onions
1   cup vinaigrette
6   mint leaves
     seasoning

Method

Clean the spring onions and chop finely.
Chop the mint leaves finely.
Clean the green peppers removing the seeds.
Cut the peppers and the onions into dice.
Cut the tomatoes into quarters.
Add all ingredients together.
Season to taste.

Avocado Pear Salad

Ingredients

3   avocados
1   green chilli
½   cup vinaigrette.
     juice of 1 lemon
     seasoning

Method

Clean and chop the green chilli.
Peel and cut the avocados into cubes.
Mix all the ingredients together.
For a hotter salad, crush the chilli with ginger and garlic.
Season to taste.

Cucumber Salad

Ingredients

1   cucumber
1   green chilli
½   cup vinaigrette
     seasoning

Method

Clean the cucumber by removing the peel and seeds.
Cut into slices.
Crush the chilli with a little salt.
Add all the ingredients together.
Season to taste.

Chopped mint can be used in place of the chilli if desired.

Pineapple Salad

Ingredients

1   pineapple
1   green chilli
30 g sugar
½ cup vinaigrette
    little water

Method

Clean and slice the pineapple.
Proceed as directed for cucumber salad.

Mango Salad

Ingredients

6   green mangoes
2   green chillies
1   slice onion
1   cup vinaigrette

Method

Proceed as for cucumber salad.

Cabbage Salad

Ingredients

1   cabbage
10 g caraway seeds
1   cup vinaigrette
60 g diced
      bacon (optional)
      seasoning

Method

Chop the cabbage very finely.
Add the caraway seeds.
If required, fry the bacon and add to the cabbage.
Mix all the ingredients together.
Season to taste.

Beanshoot Salad

Ingredients

120 g bean shoots
2   pattisons
2   potatoes
3   tomatoes
4   celery stalks
1   pinch nutmeg powder
1   cup vinaigrette
      seasoning

Method

Cook the pattisons and potatoes and cool under running cold water.
When cool cut into cubes.
Cut the tomatoes into quarters.
Clean and cut the celery into 4 cm pieces.
Add all the ingredients to the vinaigrette.
Season to taste.

Pattison Salad

Ingredients

4 pattisons
1 onion
1 boiled egg
1 cup vinaigrette
   seasoning

Method

Proceed as for beetroot salad (page 146).

Young Corn Salad

Ingredients

1   cucumber
12 young corn shoots.
2   cooked beef sausages
2   tomatoes
4   celery stalks
1   cup vinaigrette
    seasoning

Method

Peel the cucumber, remove the seeds and cut into
small cubes.
Cut the young corn shoots and sausages into slices.
Cut the tomatoes into quarters.
Clean and cut the celery into 1 cm pieces.
Add all the ingredients to the vinaigrette.
Season to taste.

Chou Chou Salad

Ingredients

3 chou chou
1 onion
1 hard boiled egg
1 cup vinaigrette
   seasoning

Method

Clean and cook the chou chou in seasoned boiling
water.
Clean and cut the onion into slices.
Peel and slice the hard boiled egg.
When cooked, cool the chou chou under cold water
and peel.
Cut into cubes.
Mix all the ingredients together adding the egg
last so as not to break slices.
Season to taste.

Beetroot Salad

Ingredients

4 beetroots
1 potato
1 onion
1 boiled egg
1 cup vinaigrette
   seasoning

Method

Cook the potato and beetroots in boiling water.
When cooked, cool under running cold water.
Peel the potato and beetroots and cut into slices.
Cut the egg into slices.
Add all the ingredients together and fold in the vinaigrette.
Season to taste.
Chop some spring onions and sprinkle on top of the salad.

Capitaine Fish Salad

Ingredients

250 g fillet of capitaine
1   chopped onion
1   cup mayonnaise
1   tablespoon tomato sauce
3   drops tabasco
     juice of one orange plus
        segments of one orange
1   tot brandy
     seasoning

Method

Poach the capitaine and allow it to cool.
Cut the capitaine into large dice.
Mix all the ingredients together.
Season to taste.

Carrot and Caraway Salad

Ingredients

4 grated carrots
1 finely sliced cabbage
1 finely sliced onion
1 cup vinaigrette
5 g caraway seeds
   seasoning

Method

Mix all the ingredients together into the vinaigrette. Season to taste.

Ham and Pineapple Salad

Ingredients

60 g diced ham
1   diced pineapple
60 g diced cheese
250 ml fresh cream
     juice of 1 lemon
30 g peanuts

Method

Mix ham, cheese, pineapple and peanuts together. Squeeze the juice of a lemon over the salad. Fold in the cream, enough to bind the ingredients together.
Season to taste.

French Beans and Potato Salad

Ingredients

250 g French beans
250 g celery
1   hard boiled egg
6   black olives
2   tomatoes
1   chilli
1   cup vinaigrette
4   boiled potatoes
    seasoning

Method

Cut the celery, potatoes and French beans into large dice.
Separate white from the hard boiled egg and chop into dice.
Cut the tomatoes into six.
Chop the chilli very finely.
Mix all the ingredients together in the vinaigrette.
Season to taste.

Desserts

straight from the sugar bowl

It comes as no surprise that the inhabitants of the 'sugar-bowl isle' should delight in sweets, cakes and desserts. As soon as the Mauritian child has teeth strong enough, he is biting into the hard, stringy stem of the cane and sucking out its sugary juices. Over 90% of cultivated land is sugar. The rolling plains and steep mountain sides sway with it. It even grows interspersed between the houses in towns and villages. Battered lorries, ambling oxcarts and local cups of tea and coffee are full of it.

Sugar has been at the heart of Mauritian history. The Dutch planted it, the African slaves cut it, the French extracted it, the Indians saved it, the British bought it, contemporary Mauritius could not survive without it. The cane plant grows to about ten feet, topped with a pale feathery flower. It is planted once in about five years. It is cut by hand between June and December. Fine white sugar is produced in 21 factories. 500,000 tons of it goes to the European Economic Community, and any extra is sold on the world market. 85% of all foreign exchange earnings come from the sugar industry — one of the most highly developed in the world.

An appreciable proportion, 40,000 tons, is consumed locally. Some of it is turned into rums and cane spirits, some goes into the making of a wide range of fizzy drinks, beer and cider. Both hard and soft drinks are manufactured under licence from international companies. Rum is popular at all social levels, from the simple behind-the-shop boozer who knocks it back down a throat of iron, to the chic consumer who gently gets sozzled on an evening in or out. Soft drinks too are consumed by all in gigantic quantities. In the old days, the poor man's drink cum dessert was *dilo dissic*, sugar water. Nowadays colas, with their trendy names, bottles and advertising image, have taken its place. Tea and coffee, both grown locally, are served with generous helpings of sugar thoughtfully stirred in by the maker beforehand.

The sugar (and rum) which is not drunk goes into sweets, cakes and desserts. French type *pâtisserie* is popular, especially on Sundays when churchgoers and beachbound picnickers stop by to pick up their supply. The *napolitain* (page 159) covered in bright pink fondant is almost a national institution. It has evolved very differently from its Franco-Italian ancestor which still calls for the complications of fresh almond paste and royal icing. The Mauritian *napolitain* would hold its own on any respectable table despite its relative simplicity. *Gâteau coco* (page 155) is another popular sweet snack. It consists of fresh coconut shavings held together by sugar crystals. Although housewives do make it, it is more often seen in what are loosely called *tabagies* from where it is purchased. Grated coconut, if not the main interest, is frequently included as a supporting ingredient in Mauritian desserts.

Since the home oven is largely alien, Indian cuisine has developed a tradition of deep-fried sweets. This tradition flourishes here. Toffee apples, dholl fritters and coconut pastries (page 151, 152, 159) involve frying rather than baking. Deep-fried sweets can be bought off the streets, so fiery that you need bits of newspaper to avoid blistering your fingertips.

Caramelised custards and tropical fruit, mixtures lit by liberal lashings of rum, dishes combining cardamom, raisins and peanuts or summer-fresh fruit salads, this is how a Mauritian meal will come to a close. The entire experience, varied and intriguing, will make the next beginning worth waiting for.

Toffee Apples

Ingredients

2   eating apples
1   egg lightly beaten
250 g sugar
1   tablespoon oil
100 g flour
1½   cups water
50   g sesame seeds
     iced water
     oil for deep frying

Method

Peel apples, core and cut into eight pieces.
Combine the lightly beaten egg with the water and
flour. This should make a fairly thick, smooth batter.
Heat the oil for deep frying.
Place the sugar, one tablespoon of oil and one cup of
water in a pan. Mix well and bring to the boil.
Cook until of a light caramel colour.
Add the sesame seeds to the caramel.
Simmer a little until it forms a thick toffee, but is not
too dark a colour. If the sugar is too dark a bitter
taste will result.
Coat the apple with the batter and place into the hot oil.
Fry to a golden brown.
Lift the apple out of the oil and place it into the
sesame toffee mix.
Turn the apple in the toffee and remove from the
toffee straight into iced water.
This will harden the toffee around the apple.
Remove from the water on to an oiled plate.
Bananas may be used in place of apples.

Dholl Fritters

Ingredients

100 g yellow lentils
1 cup coconut milk
30 g freshly
grated coconut
60 g sugar
½ teaspoon saffron powder
1 egg
water
oil for deep frying

Method

Wash the lentils well. Cover with water to about one and half inches above the level of the lentils.
Bring to the boil and cook until very soft.
Drain very well. The dholl should be of a very thick consistency.
Add the saffron powder to the sugar and blend together. Add to the dholl.
Stir into the dholl the grated coconut, sugar and milk, and let cool.
Form small balls in the palm of your hand with the dholl mixture.
If the dholl is not firm enough add a little cornflour.
Make a paste with the flour, egg, salt and water.
Beat to make a smooth batter.
Leave to stand for twenty minutes.
Heat oil to smoking point, then lower the heat.
Drop the dholl balls into the batter.
Lift out with a fork and allow batter to drain a little.
Drop the battered dholl into the oil and fry to a golden brown.
Remove and drain well.
Serve hot.
The dholl fritters can also be rolled in caster sugar when cooked.

Caramel Bananas

Ingredients

6   bananas
100 g sugar
½   cup white wine
2   tots rum
50   g butter
30   g icing sugar
1   tot curaçao
     zest and juice of 1
        orange
     zest and juice of 1
        lemon

Method

Bake bananas in oven until skin is black.
Remove from the oven.
Place butter, icing sugar, lemon, orange and curaçao
in a bowl.
Whisk until a very light cream.
Place sugar in pan and caramelize to a very light
golden brown.
Add the white wine, very carefully because the
sugar will bubble.
Stir in the wine, until it is combined into the caramel.
Remove from the heat.
Add the butter mix to the sugar and stir in well.
Remove the peel from the bananas very carefully.
Place into the sugar and reheat very gently.
Add the rum and curaçao.
When hot serve on a dish with the sauce over the
bananas.
If you want to flambé the dish, warm another tot of
rum and light.
Pour over the bananas and serve whilst flaming.

Crème Savannah

Ingredients

5   eggs
½   litre milk
150 g sugar
     water

Method

Place 125 g of sugar in a clean pan and cover with just sufficient water.
Stir to dissolve the sugar in the water.
Place on a fierce heat and bring to the boil.
When the sugar begins to turn a light caramel colour remove from the heat.
Place the pan in a bowl of cold water to stop further cooking.
Be careful of this operation as the water bubbles with heat from the pan.
Keep one quarter of the caramel apart.
Beat the eggs and the milk together and strain.
Pour this mixture into three quarters of the now darker caramel mix. Mix well.
Pour into a dish and cook in a very slow oven.
It is best to put the dish in a tray of water and then into the oven. This prevents the egg custard from getting too hot and thus boiling.
When the egg custard is set remove from the oven and allow it to cool.
Add a little water to the remaining caramel and place on a low heat.
Stir until sugar and water are mixed well together.
Care must be taken not to burn the sugar.
Remove the egg custard from the dish and turn on to a platter.
Pour over the remaining caramel.
Sprinkle the remaining sugar on the top.
Place under a very hot grill until the sugar starts to brown.
Remove and serve immediately.

Banana Cakes

Ingredients

10	bananas
200 g	arrowroot
150 g	sugar
3	cups water
5	cups thick coconut milk (page 79)
1	pinch salt
	green colour
	banana leaf

Method

Bake bananas in their skins for eight minutes.
Set aside to cool.
Place arrowroot, sugar and salt in a pan.
Stir in the milk and water and a little green colour.
Bring to the boil, stirring continuously so as not to burn.
Cook on a slow heat until the paste begins to thicken.
Peel and slice the bananas.
Cut the banana leaf into 15 cm squares.
Place a spoonful of the arrowroot mixture in the middle of each square.
Add two thick slices of banana and cover with a little more mixture.
Fold the leaf around the mixture to form a square shape. Secure with a toothpick.
Place in the refrigerator to cool and set completely.
Serve wrapped in the leaf. Aluminium foil may be used instead of the banana leaf, but the presentation is not so effective.

Gâteau Coco

Ingredients

1	grated fresh coconut
500 g	sugar
1	cup water
1	tablespoon honey
200 g	butter

Method

Place the water and honey into a pan.
Add the sugar and stir well.
Bring to boil until the sugar starts to go light brown.
When ready take the sugar off the heat.
Fold in the coconut and butter. Stir well.
Pour into a greased pan and let the mixture cool.
Cut into cubes when ready to serve.

Chocolate and Rum Mousse

Ingredients

4   egg whites
250 g sugar
125 g dark chocolate
2   tots rum
1   teaspoon cocoa

Method

Place the chocolate in a bowl and melt over warm water.
Do not let any of the water get into the chocolate.
Whisk the egg whites to a snow in a very clean bowl. Add the cocoa slowly.
Add the sugar slowly, whisking all the time.
Pour the melted chocolate into the egg whites very carefully, folding it in with your hand or a wooden spatula all the time.
Add the rum and again fold this into the chocolate mix.
Pour into champagne glasses.
Allow to set for thirty minutes in the refrigerator.

Rum Cake

Ingredients

120 g softened butter
180 g plain flour
4   eggs
240 g sugar
3   tots dark rum
30   g cornflour
10   g baking powder
      zest and juice of 3 limes

Method

Pre-heat the oven to a moderate heat 180°C.
Butter and flour a 20 cm cake tin.
Sieve together the cornflour, flour and baking powder.
Cream the butter and sugar together.
Beat well until light and fluffy.
Beat in the eggs one at a time, beating well all the time.
Add the rum and the grated lime zest and juice.
Continue beating to a smooth cream.
Fold the flour into the creamed butter and sugar mix.
Beat well continuously.
Pour the cake mix into the cake tin.
Place in the middle of the oven for approximately one hour.
Cool the cake before removing it from the tin.

Vermicelli Pudding

Ingredients

750 g vermicelli
15 g vanilla essence
1 tot rum
250 g grated fresh coconut
2 litres milk
500 g sugar
250 g raisins
2 cups thick coconut milk
(page 79)

Method

Break the vermicelli into small pieces.
Place into a pan on a high heat.
Stir and keep on heat until vermicelli browns.
Take off heat. Add the milk and coconut milk.
Return to heat and bring to the boil.
Add the sugar, grated coconut and vanilla essence.
Cook until vermicelli is soft and the mixture thickens.
Add the rum and raisins and stir well.
Pour mixture out into a greased dish and sprinkle
with more grated coconut.
Let it cool and then cut into diamond shapes.

Maize Pudding

Ingredients

2 pkts maize powder
2 litres milk
800 g sugar
10 g vanilla essence
200 g raisins
100 g grated fresh coconut
1 cup thick coconut milk
(page 79)

Method

Bring milk, coconut milk and vanilla to the boil.
Add the maize and stir well.
Cook until fairly thick.
Add the coconut, sugar and raisins and stir in well.
Cook for half a minute.
Pour into a greased dish and let it set.
When cold, cut into slices.

Semolina Cake

Ingredients

200 g fine semolina
6   cups milk
2   cups thick coconut milk
     (page 79)
2   eggs
15   g roasted sesame seeds
35   g roasted peanuts
2   black cardamoms,
        ground
500 g sugar
40   g raisins

Method

Place the semolina in a pan.
Cook over a moderate heat until a light golden brown.
Stir frequently to prevent the semolina from burning.
Remove from the heat and allow to cool.
Pour the milk and coconut milk into another saucepan.
Place on a moderate heat.
Beat the eggs and sugar together until light and smooth.
Stir in the cardamoms and peanuts.
Pour the heated milk over the cooled semolina and add the raisins.
Cook on a fairly low heat until very thick.
Stir frequently to prevent burning.
Blend the egg batter mix into the semolina.
Pour into a square greased cake tin 25 cm square.
Sprinkle the roasted sesame seeds on top.
Cover with aluminium foil and place the cake tin into a pan with a little water.
Place in moderate oven and cook for one and a quarter hours.

When cooked, leave to cool. When cold cut into diamond shaped pieces.

Napolitain

Ingredients

500 g flour
400 g butter
5 g salt
red jam
pink fondant

Method

Make a paste with the butter, flour and salt.
Roll paste out carefully and cut into 7.5 cm circles.
Take extra care with this pastry as it crumbles very
easily.
Place on to a greased tray and cook in a moderate
oven (180°C).
Do not colour when cooking.
Warm the fondant until runny but thick enough to
coat one's finger.
When the biscuits are cooked remove from the oven
and place them on to racks to cool.
Take half of the circular biscuits and spread some red
jam in the middle.
Place the other half on top.
Melt some of the red jam and brush the top of each
biscuit.
Pour over the pink fondant so that the top and sides
are covered. Leave it to set.
Remove from the rack and trim the fondant.

Coconut Pastries

Ingredients

200 g brown sugar
6 cups water
500 g rice flour
3 teaspoons baking powder
1 pinch salt
250 g grated fresh coconut
2 eggs
oil for deep frying

Method

Place the water in a pan and warm to blood heat.
Add the sugar to the water and dissolve, allow to go
cold.
Sieve together the flour, baking powder and salt.
Add the sugar water and beat to a smooth paste.
Add the grated coconut.
Whisk in the eggs to complete the batter.
Allow to stand for ten minutes.
Heat the oil to smoking point and lower the heat.
Drop in large spoonfuls of the batter.
Fry to a golden brown.
Remove and drain well.
Serve hot.

Gâteau Pistache

Ingredients for the sponge

9   eggs
320 g sugar
330 g flour
20   g crushed roasted
      peanuts

Method for the sponge

Place eggs and sugar in a bowl and warm over a very low heat, whisking all the time.
Remove from the heat after one minute.
Whisk continuously.
Sieve together the flour and the crushed peanuts.
Grease a tray 45 cm × 25 cm.
When the eggs and sugar are firm, or when the mixture keeps its shape when moved, fold in gently the flour and crushed peanuts.
Continue folding in either with the hand or a wooden spoon until all the flour is blended in.
Pour on to greased tray, level out and bake in a moderate oven.

Ingredients for the buttercream

125 g butter
125 g sugar
90 g crushed roasted
peanuts
water
red jam

Method for the buttercream

Place the sugar and sufficient water just to cover it in a very clean pan.
Stir to dissolve the sugar in the water.
Place on a fierce heat and boil for approximately three minutes.
When a spoon is placed into the sugar and straight into cold water the sugar on the spoon should roll into a soft ball.
Remove from the heat and pour into a mixer.
Whisk to cool.
When sugar is very cool add the softened butter slowly.
Whisk continuously until all the butter is added.
Whisk for a further five minutes adding the peanuts.
The buttercream should be very fluffy and light.

Finishing the gâteau

Cut the sponge into three.
(This has already been cooked and should now be cold.)
On the first layer spread the red jam.
Place the second layer on top of the jam.
Spread some buttercream on to the second layer.
Place the top layer over the buttercream.
Cover with more buttercream and decorate as desired, preferably with chopped peanuts.
Cut into slices, refrigerate for thirty minutes and serve.

Cocktails

part of a sundrenched habitat

The cocktail is as natural a part of a sundrenched habitat as orchids amidst the jungle undergrowth. The subtle blending of fragrances and flavours, of fresh fruit and fiery juices, of powerful punch and gentle persuasion, captures the essence of tropicana itself — all in a long cool sip.

The island of Mauritius is in fact one big conglomerate cocktail with its fascinating blend of races, cultures and climes; its contrast of quiet translucent lagoons and brash silver beaches, of blazing noons and cool starbright evenings; its combination of primitive simplicity and perfect sophistication.

The cocktails we include use local ingredients as *matières premières*, but are expanded and enhanced for international tastes. Mauritius turns a tiny fraction of its cane sugar into top

quality rum in the high style of Bacardi and the better Puerto Rican brews. Rum derivatives like cane spirit, coco, daïquiri and negrita punches are also produced. Gin and vodka are distilled according to international recipes and bear well-known brand names. All these liquors loom large in the concoctions that follow.

So do tropical fruit — bananas, watermelon, coconut, pineapple, pawpaw. Pawpaw or papaya grows in India, China, Tahiti, West Africa and the Indian Ocean Islands. Its soft orange flesh is sweet, and very rich in vitamins and enzymes. Use fresh pineapple rather than the tinned variety — the latter being as unacceptable as plastic flowers in the hair of a native beauty. Fresh tropical fruits have a compatibility with liquors that few substitutes can rival.

At the decorative stage, fruit and flowers come together to add the crowning aura of exoticism to the proceedings. A cocktail can be served in a scooped out pineapple or a highball inserted into a fresh coconut. A hibiscus or a small anthurium placed at the rim is the final touch that will get you musing on the wonders of nature — and the mind that invented the tropical cocktail.

Our selection covers a wide range of flavours — from the sweet cherry of 'Dodo' and the sparkling orange of 'Soleil' to the potent 'Scorpion' and the tingling sourness of a 'Blue Cyclone'. 'Planter's Punch' is mild and fruity whereas 'Mauritian Pearl', with its combination of gin and chartreuse, can give terrific momentum to an evening's entertainment. Aficionados will appreciate the subtleties of 'Fire Coral', sunworshippers the minty freshness of the 'Cooler'. Whatever your preference, you'll probably never drink cola again.

Planter's Punch

Ingredients

50   ml rum
150 ml pineapple juice
50   ml lemon juice
1   dash angostura
1   teaspoon grenadine
     crushed ice

Method

Place all ingredients in a blender together with ice and blend for a few seconds.
Pour into scooped out pineapple.
Decorate with lemon and orange slices for the eyes and pineapple for the nose.

Beachcomber

Ingredients

50 ml rum
25 ml crème de banane
75 ml pineapple juice
75 ml coconut cream
    crushed ice

Method

Place all ingredients in a blender together with
crushed ice and blend for a few seconds.
Pour into a glass which is inserted into a fresh
coconut.
Decorate with maraschino cherry and cassia flower.

Blue Cyclone

Ingredients

25 ml blue caraçao
25 ml rum
25 ml cane spirit
75 ml lemon juice
75 ml pineapple juice
    dash Pastis
    crushed ice

Method

Blend all ingredients together with the crushed ice for
a few seconds. Pour into a stemmed goblet and
decorate with lemon, pawaw and cherry.

Mauritian Pearl

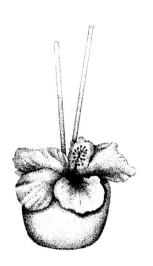

Ingredients

25 ml gin
25 ml green chartreuse
50 ml lime juice
50 ml lemon juice
    crushed ice

Method

Pour all ingredients into blender.
Blend for a few seconds.
Pour into a goblet and decorate with small
anthurium secured on a leaf with a pearl pin.

Saint Géran Passion

Ingredients

25 ml rum
25 ml coco punch
75 ml thick coconut milk
     (page 79)
75 ml pineapple juice
25 ml lime juice
     dash cinnamon
     flavoured sugar syrup
     crushed ice

Method

Blend all ingredients together and pour into
a tall glass.
Decorate with an hibiscus flower, pineapple,
pawpaw and cherry.

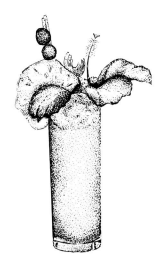

Dodo

Ingredients

50 ml rum
25 ml cherry heering
150 ml pineapple juice
     dash grenadine
     crushed ice

Method

Pour all ingredients into blender and blend
for a few seconds.
Pour into balloon glass and decorate with
cucumber and lemon slices.

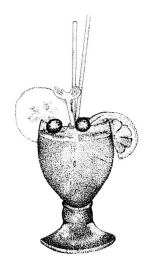

Soleil Saint Géran

Ingredients

20   ml Cointreau
25   ml Advocaat
150 ml sparkling orange
     crushed ice

Method

Stir all ingredients slowly together and pour
into tall glass.
Garnish with orange slice, pawpaw and
maraschino cherry.
Decorate with cocktail umbrella.

Fire Coral

Ingredients

50   ml rum
12.5 ml cherry heering
25   ml apricot brandy
     dash grenadine
150 ml pineapple juice
25   ml lime juice
     crushed ice

Method

Pour all ingredients into a blender with crushed ice.
Serve in a tall glass garnished with whole pine-
apple slice and segment of watermelon.
Decorate with an hibiscus.

Paul and Virginie

Ingredients

25 ml cane spirit
25 ml Galliano
75 ml orange juice
74 ml pineapple juice

Method

Pour all ingredients into shaker with six
ice cubes.
Mix for a few seconds.
Pour into a zombi glass.
Decorate with orange slice, pawpaw segment and
maraschino cherry.

Banana Daiquiri

Ingredients

25 ml rum
75 ml banana cream
25 ml crème de banane
50 ml lemon juice
   crushed ice

Method

Pour all ingredients into a blender and
blend for a few seconds.
Pour into a rolypoly glass and decorate with
banana slice, watermelon and maraschino cherry.
Decorate with an hibiscus.

Island Scorpion

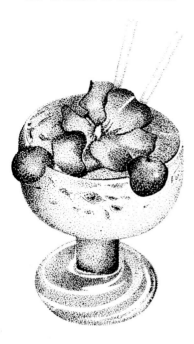

Ingredients

25 ml crème de cacao
25 ml crème de banane
25 ml coco punch
50 ml coconut cream
6   ice cubes

Method

Pour all ingredients into a cocktail shaker and shake for five seconds.
Pour into a short-stemmed goblet and decorate with sliced banana, watermelon and cherry.

Emerald Cooler

Ingredients

25 ml rum
25 ml green crème de menthe
75 ml orange juice
75 ml lemon juice
    crushed ice

Method

Pour all ingredients into blender and blend for a few seconds.
Pour into a long glass and decorate with orange, pineapple and lemon slices, together with a cherry and a mint leaf.

Metric Tables

Solid measures

In this book, quantities are given in metric measures. Exact conversion from metric into imperial measures does not give convenient working quantities (28.35 grams in 1 ounce), so the conversions given here are based on a system of 25 gram units.

Metric	Imperial
25 g	1 oz
50 g	2 oz
75 g	3 oz
100 g	4 oz (¼ lb)
150 g	5 oz
175 g	6 oz
200 g	7 oz
225 g	8 oz (½ lb)
250 g	9 oz
275 g	10 oz
300 g	11 oz
350 g	12 oz (¾ lb)
375 g	13 oz
400 g	14 oz
425 g	15 oz
450 g	16 oz (1 lb)
475 g	17 oz
500 g	18 oz
550 g	19 oz
575 g	20 oz (1 ¼ lb)
700 g	24 oz (1 ½ lb)
900 g	36 oz (2 ¼ lb)

Liquid measures

It is important to adjust the proportions of liquid and solid ingredients equally. A similar system of 25 millilitre units has therefore been used for liquid measure conversions instead of an exact fluid ounce (28.41 ml).

Metric	Imperial
25 ml	1 fl oz
50 ml	2 fl oz
75 ml	3 fl oz
100 ml	4 fl oz
150 ml	5 fl oz (¼ pt)
175 ml	6 fl oz
200 ml	7 fl oz
225 ml	8 fl oz
250 ml	9 fl oz
275 ml	10 fl oz (½ pt)
300 ml	11 fl oz
350 ml	12 fl oz
375 ml	13 fl oz
400 ml	14 fl oz
425 ml	15 fl oz (¾ pt)
450 ml	16 fl oz
475 ml	17 fl oz
500 ml	18 fl oz
550 ml	19 fl oz
575 ml	20 fl oz (1 pt)
850 ml	30 fl oz (1 ½ pt)
1000 ml	35 fl oz (1 ¾ pt)

Metric spoon measures

1 teaspoon	5 ml
1 tablespoon	15 ml

Linear Measures

Metric	Imperial
.5 cm	¼ in
1 cm	½ in
2.5 cm	1 in
5 cm	2 in
7.5 cm	3 in
10 cm	4 in
12.5 cm	5 in
15 cm	6 in
17.5 cm	7 in
20 cm	8 in
22.5 cm	9 in
25 cm	10 in

Oven temperatures

Temperature	Celcius	Fahrenheit	Gas mark
Very cool	110°C	225°F	¼
	120°C	250°F	
Cool	140°C	275°F	1
	150°C	300°F	2
Moderate	160°C	325°F	3
	180°C	350°F	4
Fairly hot	190°C	375°F	5
	200°C	400°F	6
Hot	220°C	425°F	7
	230°C	450°F	8
Very hot	240°C	475°F	9
	260°C	500°F	10

Glossary

Ajinomoto or Monosodium Glutamate
Crystals or powder, used to highlight
flavours.

Allspice A West Indian spice of the myrtle
family. It has a flavour resembling a combination of the nutmeg, cloves and mace. Its
pods are similar to peppercorns in
appearance. Not to be confused with mixed
spice which is a blend of the sweet spices.

Anis Is used in savoury and sweet cooking. It
has a light liquorice flavour. Caraway seed
may be used as an alternative.

Banana leaves Use young pale green leaves.
Used as fragrant wrappers for roasting or
steaming food. Soften the leaves by plunging
into boiling water or holding over a flame.
Grease lightly to prevent food sticking.
Aluminium foil may be used as a substitute.

Basil Pungent herb used in flake, powdered
or fresh form.

Bay leaves Often used dried and are a
traditional ingredient of the bouquet garni.
The berries of the bay tree are used in the
distillation of the spirit of aromatic herbs
called Floravanti.

BBQ sauce A sweet red brown sauce made
with garlic, spices, soya beans and chillies.
Known also as Hoisin sauce.

Béarnaise Sauce A French sauce made with
shallots, chervil or tarragon, cooked in white
wine or vinegar, and thickened with butter
and egg yolks.

Beignet French name for fruit, vegetable or
cheese dipped in batter and deep fried.

Bilimbie A bitter fruit grown in Mauritius.
Two different types are grown; the round
bilimbie is the size of a grape; the long
bilimbie grows to a length of 5 cm.

Cardamom Available in two forms, black or
green. The black seeds come in large pods,
which contain clusters of seeds and are used
as an important curry spice in garam masala
and also as fragrant spice in sweets. The
smaller greenish pods have a mild lemon
fragrance and are also used as a sweet or
savoury spice. Can also be bought in powder
form.

Chinese mushrooms Dried black Chinese
mushrooms should be soaked and softened
before use. Japanese shiitake are similar in
appearance, but have a totally different
flavour.

Cinnamon Used in sweet and savoury
cooking; sold also in powder form. Stick
cinnamon keeps the flavour longer.
Originates from Sri Lanka. Cassia is similar
to cinammon but has a much coarser
flavour.

Coriander Used extensively in Mauritian
cookery. The leaves, sometimes known as
Chinese parsley, have a strong and distinctive
flavour. Also available as seeds.

Court bouillon A simple court bouillon for
fish is salted water, sliced onions, vinegar,
bay leaf, chopped carrots, parsley, thyme,
peppercorns and a little white wine.

Cumin Black is more peppery than white.
White a totally different spice. A seed

resembling caraway but with a completely different flavour. Another important ingredient in garam masala. Used whole or in powder form in most spicy dishes.

Curry leaf   A fragant leaf that no curry should be without. May be used dry but the fresh leaf is far superior.

Curry paste   A commercially prepared paste containing the curry spices, using oil or coconut milk as a base.

Fenugreek   The fresh leaves are often used as a vegetable in India. Dried seeds smell of burnt sugar and have a slightly bitter taste.

Fruits de Cythie   A fruit that is used when green and bitter for achards and chutney. When ripe, it may be eaten as a fruit.

Garam masala   A blend of spices prepared as a curry paste or as a condiment for Indian cooking. Unlike curry powder does not contain chilli powder or turmeric. Keeps for up to one month in an airtight container.

Ghee   Clarified butter used as the main medium for Indian cooking. Vegetable oil may be substituted. Has a high cholesterol count.

Ginger juice   Used as a marinade or seasoning ingredient. Grate the root ginger and squeeze the juice through muslin.

Julienne   Finely shredded vegetables or meat.

Lentils or Dholl   Dried beans and peas used in many Mauritian dishes to make vegetarian meals, sauce and sweet and savoury snacks also known as dholl.

Mange tout   A sugar pea of which the pod is eaten as well as the seeds.

Marjoram   This aromatic herb is used in cookery from the flower labiate.

Mee Foon   Very fine threads of rice vermicelli. When deep fried they puff up and become very crisp. Also used in soups.

Mine   Also known as egg or Chinese noodles.

Natural Yoghurt   Used extensively in Indian cooking to enrich the food.

Rice   Basmati and Patna are the best known types of long grain rice.

Root ginger   Essential in most Mauritian dishes. Dried ginger is no substitute. Fresh ginger should be peeled or scraped and the flesh finely shredded or grated.

Rosemary   The leaves of this evergreen are used extensively for seasoning, fresh or dried. The leaves are narrow, green and hard with a strong aromatic smell.

Saffron   Powdered and strand saffron are commonly used for a delicate flavour and a bright orange-yellow colour.

Sesame oil   Used in Chinese cooking to give a nutty aroma and rich flavour. Made from sesame seeds and is a dark brown oil. Use with other oils as it burns at a low temperature and has a very strong taste.

Sesame seeds   High in protein, white sesame seeds are used as a garnish and are often roasted.

Soya sauce   Dark soya is used when sauces and meats need that extra colour. Not as salty as the light soya.

Tamarind   Flesh from the seed pods of the tamarind tree, grown extensively in Mauritius. Mix with hot water to make a strong flavoured acidulating liquid. Vinegar, lime or lemon juice mixed with a little water can be used as a substitute. Used extensively in Madras cooking.

Turmeric   Bright yellow spice which has a musky fragrance and a distinctive flavour. Powdered turmeric is stronger than fresh. Used for colouring and flavouring many curry and rice dishes.

Index to Dishes

Acknowledgements

Many people and organizations have given generous assistance in the compilation and illustration of this book. Since a complete list would require several pages to reproduce, acknowledgements are limited to the following:

Mr S Boyjonauth
Mr A Hosany
Mrs M Masson
Mr F Muir
Mr B N Nathan
Mr S Peerally
Mr R Phillips
Mrs A Ramtohul
Mr A Slome
Mr V Sooklall
Southern Sun Hotel Corporation

We thank the publishers of the following materials which were used as references:
Paul & Virginie by Bernardin de St Pierre (1838, l'Edition Curmer).
Mauritius: Former Isle de France (1979, Les Editions de Cygne) by P. Lenoir.
They Came to Mauritius (1965, OUP) — D Hollingworth.
Kreol (1972, C. Hurst & Co) by P. Baker.
Golden Bats and Pink Pigeons by Gerald Durrell (1977, William Collins Sons & Co Ltd.)
Pages Choisies d'Auteurs Mauriciens (1968) Ed. by C de Rauville et J. Tsang Mang Kin.
Cooking from the Commonwealth — Robin Howe (1958, Deutch)
Larousse Gastronomique

PAUL JONES & BARRY ANDREWS